To my own 'little platoon',

Never yet a monstrous regiment

Contents

Preface

This is a book about the Conservative party, led back into government by David Cameron in May 2010. The formation of a new government after 13 years of opposition can be signalled as a new politics. Partly, this is because the party can now put behind it nearly 20 years of dispute, controversy and failure and take real decisions again. But the political situation is also new because we have a coalition government, with the Conservatives in partnership with the Liberal Democrats. This certainly seems new. Cameron and his colleagues have made the most of this situation, suggesting that the Coalition will be progressive in its actions and offer radical change. This is consistent with much of the rhetoric of the Conservatives since Cameron's election as leader in late 2005.

However, my method in considering the newness of Conservative politics is to look backwards. It is my argument that we can only explain what has happened, and is happening, in Conservative politics by trying to locate these events within the history of the party and conservatism[1] more generally. We can portray politics as being concerned with reacting to change. Of course, the Conservatives can be seen as the party that resists change: that conserves rather than reforms. But this is a rather simplistic view.

Perhaps the greatest of all conservative thinkers was Edmund Burke, and what makes him so is his profound understanding of the place of change and reform in society. Burke argued that a society does not stand still. This is not because he concurred with a progressive agenda or saw change as a virtue. Indeed, Burke believed quite the opposite. He wished to preserve much of society as it was, but he saw that change was inevitable. All societies, in Burke's time and ours, are continually being buffeted by events: wars happen despite the best attempts to maintain peace; we have to respond to natural disasters and to acts of violence and terrorism; the economy changes in ways we cannot predict; and so on. Governments are constantly faced with the unforeseen and the unpredictable and they have to react: doing nothing, therefore, might not always be a terribly sensible option.

Burke argued that any society needs to have the means to create change. However, this was not because he saw any great virtue in progress or had a particular vision for where he wished Britain and its Empire to move towards. Instead he argued that no state could preserve itself unless it had the means to change. Preservation is not about standing still, but being able to bend enough as the need demands. Burke did see great virtue in Britain just as it was then, and this was precisely because this was how it had been able to evolve without any great external intervention for several hundred years. It is only by being able to change that we can preserve those institutions – such as the rule of law, free markets and private property – that make our society what it is. We need to be able to respond to the unpredictable and the unforeseen, not to fulfil some utopian vision, but to conserve what we hold dear and see as being fundamentally important to us. Burke sought to conserve certain important institutions and traditions and he realised that this involved a process of evolution, not towards any particular end – a society does not become more perfect than it already is – but in order to maintain itself and the people it contains. Importantly for Burke, these people included not just those currently within that society, but also those who were now dead and those yet to be born. We have been left certain institutions by those who came before us and we have a duty to pass them on to those who follow. In this way we honour those who have created what we now enjoy. But this, in turn, presses a duty on us to conserve what makes our society what it is.

So what matters most is not change itself, but how we respond to it. Do we seek to plan and reform to make our society better? Do we believe we can control and understand what might happen in the future, so that change becomes risk-proof? Do we take the view that change is worth the risk of losing or altering fundamentally what we now have and know? Do we find the hypothetical – the promise of the new – exciting and invigorating, or are we risk-averse and prefer the tried and trusted precisely because it is known? In other words, do we look forward or backwards? Do we seek to create our future, or do we seek to preserve the present?

So we can use the past to help us understand the present, and in doing so we should not lose sight of the irony that what we are considering here is a party and a government that claims to be progressive. The Conservative party wishes to put its past behind it, to prove it has changed, and so be given the opportunity to lead the country to a brighter, less debt-ridden future. However, it is not necessarily my aim to be critical of what the Conservatives are doing. Rather I shall contend that what Cameron has done is largely consistent with what the Conservative party has done in the past, and with what conservatives like Burke would have advised them to do.

But we still have a problem. The obvious corollary of wishing to be seen as progressive, as the Conservatives now describe themselves, is that we see reaction and tradition in particularly pejorative terms. To call someone a reactionary is perhaps one of the worst possible insults in contemporary political discourse. It might not be as bad as being called a racist, but it is still pretty bad.

Being a conservative I am sometimes referred to as a reactionary. This is, of course, intended as a criticism, as a knockdown argument to end any debate. I have been put in my place, found out, unmasked and no more needs to be said, other than for me to admit my guilt. My response is normally simply to say 'Thank you'. Indeed I am more than happy to bear the label of reactionary. I would suggest that most of us, to a greater or lesser extent, are reactionaries. Quite simply, reacting is what we do. This, it might be argued, is not exactly what the critic intended. The term for them is loaded with significance; for them it implies obscurantism, being out of touch, outdated and preposterous. Yet the word has a root, and that root is about responding to a stimulus – you prick me and I react: something happens and it causes a response. The response might be different in proportion and effect, but what matters initially here is that we react to a stimulus. So what we do is react and this applies at the basic everyday level and at the level of high politics.

It might be argued that this reduces the concept of reaction to a banality, a commonplace, and so drains it of any significance. Critics of reaction, however, are being more specific and using it only to refer to a particular attitude or form of politics. But my view is precisely the opposite: seeing reaction as a very generalised action shows just how far political reaction is grounded in natural responses. One of the purposes of this book is to demonstrate how ingrained this sense of reaction is.

I see no problem in using the label of reactionary. Partly this is because I see nothing difficult in associating myself with writers like Edmund Burke and Joseph de Maistre. But it is also because I see the concepts of reaction and reacting as being much wider than might be commonly formulated. I believe, and I shall argue for this throughout this book, that reaction is what much of practical politics consists of: politics is not so much about planning but about reacting, and recognition of this is very important. Indeed it is this recognition that makes Burke such a seminal figure in political thought.

Burke and de Maistre are the main influences on this work, and I have returned continually to their works in the preparation and writing of this book. Their books now seem like reliable old friends who I never tire of seeing again, and in whose company I always feel comfortable yet invigorated. It is my view that there is much to be gleaned from a careful study of these thinkers and this applies particularly to the art of policy making. For both Burke and de Maistre policy making was a matter of reacting to circumstance and events, of calculating where we now are and what impact this might have for civil society.

Accordingly, they promulgated responses based on this calculation rather than on some abstract set of principles. This, I hope will come across in my discussions of Conservative policies of both the Thatcher and Cameron eras.

But I have some more practical debts to acknowledge as well. First, I need to thank the support for this project offered by Emily Watt and her colleagues at The Policy Press. The development of this project was a tortuous one, not helped by the fluidity of politics in 2009 and 2010, and Emily was wonderfully supportive in getting this project off the ground and keeping it flying. Second, I continue to be humbled by the generosity and support offered by my colleagues within the Centre for Comparative Housing Research at De Montfort University. I am fortunate to work in an environment which is both truly collegiate but which also provides the encouragement and freedom to develop one's own ideas to the full.

Despite my evident fogey-ness, and much to the amusement of my wife and daughters, I have discovered Facebook and have found it an invaluable way of sharing ideas with likeminded people from across the planet. I have bounced my ideas off friends on the 'Traditional Conservatism' page and learnt a lot from them. It may be one of the few pages on Facebook where people write in proper sentences, but then reform has to start somewhere.

Finally, and even though I am increasingly the butt of their seemingly exasperated humour, I thank my wife, B, and my daughters, Helen and Rachel, for their support, love and tolerance of one berk reading another.

Note
As a general rule I use the lower case 'c' when discussing conservatism in general and reserve the upper case 'C' for when considering the Conservative party.

Introduction

In May 2010 Britain elected a new Conservative Prime Minister, for the first time since 1992. But it did not get, properly speaking, a new Conservative government. Under David Cameron's leadership, Conservative ideas have undergone something of a resurgence in the UK. Since his election as party leader in 2005 there has been a gradual emergence of a new form of Conservatism based on the ideas of compassion, social justice and progress. This, perhaps unsurprisingly, proved to be controversial: those on the left saw it as a cynical attempt to rebrand the Conservative party and to steal the clothes of New Labour. However, many commentators on the right were, and remain, dismissive of the very idea of 'progressive conservatism' and seek a return to a more traditional model of Conservatism based on low taxes and traditional morality.

What gave ammunition to these critics is the fact that Cameron's strategy, despite a considerable improvement in vote share and seats won, was at best only partially successful. The failure in the 2010 General Election to achieve an outright majority despite the economic recession and unpopularity of Gordon Brown has called into question Cameron's modernisation agenda. How could the Conservatives not win an outright majority in the circumstances of 2010 with a record peacetime public deficit created by a government that now seemed to be tired and out of ideas? Unsurprisingly, this gave renewed force to the debate about the progressive direction of the Conservative party. If only, some argued, the party had maintained its traditional agenda of tax cuts and antipathy towards Europe it would have won handsomely. However, others more sympathetic to modernisation have suggested that Cameron actually achieved a major feat in winning nearly 100 seats from Labour and gaining a swing in the 2010 election akin to that of Margaret Thatcher in 1979. The problem for Cameron, according to this view, was not where he ended up but where he was forced to start from.

But whatever gloss is put on the outcome, the Conservatives failed to win outright and found themselves in a coalition with the Liberal Democrats, a party ostensibly of the centre-left. This was an outcome that could not have been predicted before the election and still seems implausible to many in both parties. The Liberal Democrats fear it might lead to the very demise of their party, as they become associated with Tory cuts and the unpopularity of government. Their apparent falling level of support in opinion polls since May 2010 is offered as evidence of this. The Conservatives fear a dilution of their agenda for government, something they were quite confident of putting in place when they had double-digit leads in the opinion polls in early 2010.

But there is also a view that the coalition might actually present an opportunity to develop the progressive Conservative agenda promoted by Cameron since 2005. Where there is affinity with the Liberal Democrats it is on issues such as climate change, civil liberties and decentralisation. The coalition might therefore institutionalise a genuinely new form of politics and help to fundamentally change the Conservative party (and the Liberal Democrats) for good.

The Conservative party has quite a past. It could be described as the most successful democratic political party in the world over the last 130 years (Ramsden, 1998). Since the introduction of universal suffrage in the UK it has dominated electoral politics, having ruled on its own or as the dominant member of a coalition for two-thirds of this period. However, with the electoral success of New Labour under Tony Blair this golden period seemed to be at an end. The Conservative party found itself in a long and protracted slump where it seemed unable to elect an attractive leader or come to terms with how the country had changed (Bale, 2010). It seemed to be living in the past, as if it deserved to rule by right and that somehow it was being cheated out of its proper role as the natural party of government. It was not until Cameron became leader that the party seriously began to look at itself and to question what its role in modern Britain might be (Bale, 2010; Snowdon, 2010). Cameron sought to persuade the Conservative party to look forward again – to be a party of reform – rather than focus on the past and be concerned with fighting the battles of the last war. Part of this attempt to shift the party forwards was a deliberate change in rhetoric, particularly with the use of terms such as compassion, social justice and most noticeably the idea of progressive Conservatism.

While in previous times such a phrase might have been taken for an absurdity, it is certainly the case that this notion has gained some credence in recent years (Blond, 2010). Conservative politicians indeed do claim that they are now the progressive force in British politics. This seems to be based on the assumption that to call oneself progressive is in some way desirable and perhaps even virtuous.

Accordingly, it appears that many on the right have become afraid of appearing non-progressive or reactionary. This, of course, is not how many people see Conservatism. As the name suggests, it is deemed to exist in order to conserve and to preserve certain institutions and ways of life. Conservatism, one would have thought, ought to be the very opposite of progress.

Indeed, according to the conservative philosopher, Roger Scruton (2000), the consummate conservative politician was Lord Salisbury, in that despite being Prime Minister for nearly 13 years in the late 19th and early 20th centuries, we know very little about him. The virtue of Salisbury is that he is said to have left the country pretty much as he found it. According to Scruton, 'Salisbury was animated by the knowledge that it is easier to lose good things than to create them, and that the task of politics is to understand an inheritance of laws and institutions, and to protect it from unnecessary experiment' (p 190). Salisbury's view of politics could be summed up by the phrase 'delay is life' (Scruton, 2000, p 197): our normal way of existing, and therefore of governing, is by a process of holding back change and protecting those institutions that maintain our way of life.

This view is not that change does not happen, or that it should never occur. It is, however, based on the premise that change should only occur for the right reason, and this is generally to preserve what is good about how we live. The role of the wise politician, therefore, is to understand just what contributes to making our way of life what it is and to protect it from threats.

This, doubtless to say, would be considered an eccentric idea by most modern politicians. It is more common to suggest that the purpose of politics is to promote the need for change: the role of the politician is not to keep things as they are or to preserve, but to change them. Indeed, one often does not even need to state what one wishes to change. It is merely assumed that this is what politics is about.

Barack Obama had great success in his election campaign for the US presidency merely through using the word 'change'. He did not have to say what he would be changing, merely promising to be distinct from those who had come before him and to do things differently. Obama's appeal was partly that he was so very different from his predecessor: he was a younger, black, liberal, northern man as opposed to a white, conservative Texan. He could definitely be seen as different, as definitely 'not-Bush', and so offer hope and opportunity to those disappointed, disillusioned or angered by the Bush presidency. This sense of difference meant that Obama could 'be the change' without having necessarily to spell out just what he would be changing. Indeed, it might be this very vagueness, this real lack of any detail about what might change, that was crucial to Obama's success. Such an approach has also been taken by David Cameron, and while his success is less spectacular than that of President Obama, it too has propelled him into office.

Underpinning these campaign tactics was a belief that change is always a good thing, and that it is what most people want. By implication not seeking change is taken to be a liability and a politically dangerous attitude to admit to. While some politicians might point to their experience and longevity as a selling point this does not lead them to suggest that they will keep things just as they are. They may promise steadiness and security, but the reason for this is because we live in a changing world and so a steady hand is needed to steer the ship of state through the squalls ahead. An experienced hand, it can be argued, is best at guiding us through the uncertainty of rapidly changing times.

The label which no politician would happily see adhered to them is that of 'reactionary'. This would imply that they were against change and progress; that they were backward looking and therefore taking the country in the wrong direction. Far better, it is said, to be progressive and adopt a radical agenda. Clearly, there are examples of conservatives being radical. Mrs Thatcher referred to herself on occasion as both a radical and a revolutionary (Green, 2006) and President Reagan also sought to transform America. The Republicans in 1994 successfully sought a new contract with America seeking to transform the country. Sarah Palin, the defeated Republican Vice-Presidential candidate argued in February 2010 that it was time for a new revolution in America, this time against big government. Less recently we can think of writers in the conservative tradition who have reacted violently and condemned change such as Joseph de Maistre (1974) and his criticisms of the French Revolution and Charles Maurras's strident rejection of French secular republicanism. Both de Maistre and Maurras argued against the status quo – the current state of affairs – and sought to change that state back to what they thought it had once been, to a social order that placed at its centre throne and altar rather than the nostrums of radical Enlightenment. We can also point to the elegant but no less vigorous condemnation of the French Revolution undertaken by Edmund Burke (1992, 1999b, 1999c), although in this case he was comparing the stability of the English Constitution with the upheavals and bloody violence across the Channel.

What Burke suggests is that we can seek to be resilient and strong in the face of change, even where the sense of imminent danger is very great. Conservatives like Burke felt that the stakes were very high, in terms of the importance of the institutions they saw as being threatened. Were the ideas of the French Revolution to grow roots in England they might have strangled the indigenous ideas of hierarchy and order. So it matters to conservatives that change might have a fundamental or even ruinous impact on institutions seen as crucial to a particular way of life. In this way they feel that they must act, and act positively, in order to preserve what they see as threatened. Passivity and acceptance are not options once one's way of life is endangered.

Indeed, one of Burke's most famous phrases is, 'A state without the means of some change is without the means of its conservation' (1999b, p 108). Societies which cannot adapt will tend to ossify and die. They become brittle and fall to dust. Those societies which wish to survive, and to do so on their own terms, keeping their way of life intact, must be able to shift and roll with the changing tide of events. Change is not therefore to be rejected out of hand, but instead seen as a tool that has a very specific purpose, namely that of preserving. This then is not change for its own sake, but change for a limited purpose: it is change that does not seek to transgress, but to maintain.

Burke would have us belief that any attempt at change should be seriously questioned. The reason for this is because, like Salisbury a century later, he has a somewhat pessimistic view of politics. Salisbury considered that it is easier to lose important things than to win them back or recreate them. We might call this the 'tightrope' view of politics. Experience tells us that there is only a very fine line along which we can travel and remain safe, and the consequences of moving off this line are disastrous and irreversible. It takes concentration, courage and fortitude and no little skill to retain our balance. We need to be extremely careful because we know that once we fall we cannot recover; once we have changed things such that once treasured institutions are gone they cannot be readily replaced or returned to. The old status quo cannot be rebuilt once it has been pulled apart – we cannot get back on the tightrope – and so our efforts should be put into preventing the changes from being made in the first place. This will involve us being strong-willed and determined to ignore siren calls which will break our concentration and lead to our downfall.

This Burkean position states that we delay those forces that would destroy us and so allow our institutions to adapt and re-form in a manner that leaves them, and us, intact. The aim of politics is to remain safe, to survive so we can continue on. This might not be a gentle or even a consensual process, as Mrs Thatcher found when facing down trade unions and the left in the 1980s. This is precisely because events continue to occur, and so, as much as we might wish things to remain as they are, our way of life will from time to time come under threat and we must go out and fight for it.

The situation, however, was different for a thinker like Joseph de Maistre. He had lost all he held dear: the crown, the centrality of the Church, his homeland and his birthright had all been taken from him (Lebrun, 1988). What he wanted therefore was not to preserve what existed in the present, but to return to what once was. He did not simply accept the status quo, but rather wished a radical transformation of it. This is because he saw this new state – Revolutionary and Imperial France – as illegitimate and against the natural order of things. De Maistre was not reacting to the threat of change, but seeking instead to overturn change that had already occurred. He could therefore be seen as a counter-revolutionary.

John O'Hara (2010), in his book on the tea party protests that began in reaction to President Obama's economic and health policies in 2009, draws a useful distinction between revolution and counter-revolution. O'Hara describes the US tea party protesters as counter-revolutionaries. They are fighting against a revolution they see as already under way and which is fundamentally transforming America, turning it from a country of individual freedom, low taxation and small government to a European-style social democracy. As O'Hara puts it, the protesters want their country back. They oppose the bailouts, health care reforms and cap and trade measures proposed by the Obama administration, seeing these policies as somehow alien to the American tradition. O'Hara portrays this as a genuine grassroots movement against what the protesters consider to be an over-large and over-active government. But what is particularly interesting is O'Hara's description of counter-revolution:

> [T]he movement is not and never was a revolution but a counter-revolution. This is a crucial distinction. To revolt is an attempt to break free from and overthrow a long-standing political structure. The tea parties do the opposite by opposing radical policies of bailouts, handouts, wealth re-distribution, and intrusion into our lives that can only be described as radically revolutionary. Big spending and a nanny state is radical. (2010, pp 203–4)

The tea party movement 'is about protecting individual liberty and the documents and institutions that have made it possible' (p 204, emphasis in original). He goes on:

> The tea parties and the movement they ignited aren't about a radical right-wing agenda but an American agenda. Our values are the values of the mainstream. The only radicalism involved in this movement is the preservation of the once radical ideas defended by the Founders that people should

have a right to life, liberty and the pursuit of happiness.
(p 204)

So O'Hara argues that this movement is a concern to reassert mainstream values in the face of what is perceived of as an alien threat, as something deeply inimical to the politics traditions of the USA. It is this assertion of being part of a threatened mainstream that leads de Maistre to qualify his views on revolution. He argued that his aim, the restoration of the monarchy in France, 'will not be a *contrary revolution*, but the *contrary of revolution*' (1974, p 169, emphasis in original). He is promoting the opposite of revolution, which seeks to restore what was long established but now lost.

Of course, we need not accept this particular view. After all Barack Obama, whom the tea party protesters are campaigning against, was elected with a clear majority. However, what does matter here is the self-perception of this group of ordinary people turned protesters. The tea party protesters do not see themselves as radicals or as revolutionaries. Instead they perceive themselves as working towards putting things back as they were. They are not seeking to preserve but to restore.

The tea party movement, like the 200-year-old arguments of de Maistre, are reactionary. They are seeking to counter something that is currently happening and which they profoundly dislike. We might see this protest as simplistic and negative. It tends to focus on what it is opposed to and perhaps sometimes taking for granted what it is for. They see the need to argue *against* rather than *for* something. The protesters are opposed to the current government and the so-called 'beltway consensus'. Their main argument is to call for less of things or for them to stop outright rather than putting forward the stereotypical utopian dream of the revolutionary. Their anger is directed at change that has already occurred.

So we can suggest that there are (at least) two forms of reaction: that which seeks to preserve and that which seeks to restore. What unites them is their attitude towards change. But there is a problem here. Reaction is quite properly associated with conservatism. Many of the tea party protesters may be new to political activism as O'Hara claims, but he is certainly a fully committed and active conservative and so are many of those who have become involved in supporting and promoting the protests. Burke, although the term was unknown to him, is seen as the founder of conservatism, in the English-speaking world at least. But because conservatism is rather more of a disposition than a set of ideological doctrines or principles (Scruton, 2001), it is more adaptable and ready to change than other ideologies. Conservatism can and does respond to situations without recourse to particular dogma or utopianism. As Scruton (2001) argues, conservatism is an ideology that is concerned with the surface of things and so with how life actually is lived. Therefore when change occurs, conservatives adapt to that new situation. At its heart is a ready responsiveness to change based on the overarching need to preserve important social institutions. This, of course, means that there is no particular set of policies or dogmas that are immutably conservative (Kekes, 1998). Part of the very nature of conservatism, therefore is its adaptability in the face of change. It is as much in the nature of conservatives to adapt, as it is to oppose. This will need some further teasing out if we are to fully understand conservatism.

There are those who portray conservatism, and reaction more generally, as being based on fear. Because we do not know what the future might bring we fear it and seek to hold it at bay. We oppose what we do not understand rather than coming to terms with it. Reaction is accordingly often portrayed as negative: it is backward-looking, fearful or obscure; reactionaries are seen are unpleasant types who dislike or hate things and people rather than accepting them. Indeed it is this distinction that politicians like David Cameron have used in trying to modify the image of the Conservative party. In the past the Conservatives were the 'nasty party' interested in the economy or 'hard' issues like immigration and European integration. Instead the new Conservatives wish to put across a softer image and so talk about the environment, well being and the quality of life.

What is lost in this discussion is the notion that conservatism is concerned not just with outcomes but also with attitudes: it is a way of living, and not merely a means of optimising outcomes. There is more to conservatism than just winning elections. Conservatism is also a way of looking at things and making sense of them. So we should not merely dismiss someone because they have a fear of change. This fear might be based on a genuine sense of the precariousness of life or due to experience of how difficult change can be. Indeed, what basis do we actually have to assume that what is to come will be better or preferable to what we have now? How can we possibly know? What we can know is what we have now and what that means for us, and if we feel it is fragile or at risk then is it not rational to fear its loss?

It might be argued that it is equally rational for those who are currently in dire straits to favour the future, in that it surely could not be worse than the present. The future might hold out hope for a better life and so a change from the status quo is seen as desirable. Of course, there is no certainty here, but the desperate might be prepared to gamble. This is because the future always has one great advantage over the past. As that which has not yet happened is hypothetical, the future cannot be gainsaid. It is full of possibility and, because it is currently empty, we can fill it with our dreams, hopes and desires. There is no need for limits and we need not be disappointed: that which has not yet happened cannot harm us. This might lead us to actively seek change in the prospect or hope of achieving our dreams.

But there is no certainty here and our actions are based on hope, and not on our particular circumstances. If we are dissatisfied with the present, or if we feel optimistic towards the future, we might seek change and hold out for the promise of progress. But there is no guarantee that things will be better: if they are bad now, why should they improve? What basis do we have to make claims for the future other than wishful thinking and optimism? Why, indeed, should we not take the past and present – places that we know much more about – as better guides for what might occur in the future? We know the value of certain institutions and particular ways of life. We know what we need and what currently existing institutions do and so which ones can help us fulfil these needs. But the future provides us with no such certainty. We might see some promise in progress, but ultimately we are guessing. Certainly, this might not always be a bad option to take. There are situations where we should expect to be transported to something better. But unless we can see into the future we cannot know if our guesses are based on anything substantial.

It is entirely possible that we seek change precisely because the present is familiar and so there is no sense of excitement or challenge with what we have now. Also there are those who believe in progress as an end in itself, who consider that things always can and should get better and that we should look forward with confidence because the future is likely to be an improvement on the past. Human societies always seem to develop, technology improves, production increases, and why should it stop? This being so, there is indeed no need to qualify the need for change: change is always good because societies progress.

Accordingly, for many the idea of progress needs no justification, while to be reactionary is nearly always seen as negative. One cannot describe oneself as a reactionary without people expressing a negative view or offering a sneer. The term is most often used as an insult or as a criticism. Hence to be against change or progress is always seen as wrongheaded. To look backwards is seen as regressive, negative, shallow and narrow. Reaction can never be a good thing.

But this attitude against reaction is itself based on nothing other than an attitude of mind: it has the same status as the presumption against change. There is nothing to suggest that change is necessarily always good. It is hard to see Hitler and Stalin as a positive progression on what went before, or to see Somalia or Zimbabwe as progressing to a sustainable and happy future. While over 67 million people voted for Barack Obama's clarion call for change, 58 million voted against it, and had Obama himself faced the US electorate in the November 2010 mid-term elections, after the passage of an unpopular health bill through Congress and having made little attempt to tackle a steeply rising public deficit, he would have perhaps had markedly less success in persuading the American electorate that change was really such a good idea after all.

What I wish to suggest is that the attitude that favours reaction is really quite widespread. However, unlike the idea of progress, which is seen as desirable, many people who might be called reactionaries would shy away from acknowledging themselves as such. We can see why this might be when we consider a definition of reaction. It means to be opposed to radical change. While, in practice, this need not mean being against all change many of the cognates for the term imply precisely that: we find words such as blimpish, counter-revolutionary, die-hard, obscurantist and right-winger. While the US tea party movement might happily see itself as counter-revolutionary and many might not take issue with being called 'right-wing', it is unlikely that anyone would actively seek to be called either blimpish or an obscurantist.

This perception of reaction is only heightened when one looks at the meaning of 'progressive'. This is always seen as much more positive. It relates to the desirability and possibility of change and progress, and to the idea of moral and social improvement. This clearly suggests an optimistic view of human nature, and this is further emphasised by cognates of progressive, which include avant-garde, dynamic, enlightened, forward-looking, go-ahead, liberal, modern, radical, reformist, revolutionary and up and coming. These different cognates really show the judgemental manner in which each term is held. There is a presumption that progress is good, positive, virtuous even, while to be a reactionary is seen as largely negative and even absurd.

But why should this be so? Why should those who base their ideals on the past and the present be seen as absurd and out of touch? Perhaps it is a case of the victor being able to write the history of the war. There may be something in this, but there is perhaps a more significant reason. The basis of conservatism has always been the present and the past, those concrete elements in which our everyday lives are formed. This means that conservative ideas both tend to be backward-looking and anti-theoretical (Scruton, 2001). They do no seek to build a vision for the future, but rather seek to establish the significance of the past to help us fully appreciate the present. This, however, presents conservatives and reactionaries with a problem: they have to work harder to prove their relevance.

Conservatives look to the past for their authorities. They do this by referring to traditions, but also via written authorities that they then use to validate their arguments. They might therefore look to writers such as Russell Kirk, Michael Oakeshott and Roger Scruton in recent times, or go back to Edmund Burke and Joseph de Maistre. This allows conservatives to demonstrate a certain continuity over time. We see this in English conservatives who will refer (and defer) to Burke, whose work is still quoted extensively and who is still written about (O'Keeffe, 2010). Yet there is a difficulty here, in that we now have a number of cultural, political and social institutions that these 18th-century thinkers would have seen as anathema in their own time. These might include mass immigration, the public acceptance of atheism, religious tolerance, unmarried parenting and even universal suffrage and representative democracy. They might find these developments hard to accept. Burke argued against the reform of the electoral system and took a gradualist view of religious tolerance within the context of the English Protestant settlement (1999d). Illegitimacy and atheism were not unknowns in the 18th century, but they were not acknowledged or seen as being acceptable. There existed a considerable stigma against them. Both Burke and de Maistre argued against popular democracy and sought to secure what they considered the rightful place of monarchy and aristocracy. Does this mean that they are of no use to us now? Indeed, might critics of conservatism use these anti-democratic views to tarnish modern conservatism, and if this is the case, should we not rely on more modern sources less besmirched by views we now find unacceptable and anachronistic? In other words, what use are Burke and de Maistre now and what does this suggest about look backwards for our authorities?

Ignoring the fact that Karl Marx lived nearer to the time of Burke and de Maistre than our own, and so what applies to them as out-dated thinkers might also apply to Marx, we need to appreciate an important element in conservative thinking, namely that we can only operate within the particular conditions that pertain to us at the time. Just as we look to the past for our authorities and see the conditions of today as inescapable, so did Burke and de Maistre. They argued as they did precisely because of the circumstances in which they operated within, and were they to have been brought up in our time, we would expect their conservatism to represent this. What made these thinkers conservative is not just what they argued, but *how* they argued. What is important about these writers today is not just the specifics of their arguments against revolution and radical change, but what underpins their particular positions. It is the disposition that they demonstrate and not the specific conclusions they might reach with regard to electoral reform or capital punishment. Burke is still read, not so much for the detail of his argument or for his purple prose on Marie Antoinette, but for the spirit and the general sense he provides in favour of tradition and preservation. We read him for his justifications that we should change only to preserve and protect what is dear to us. We read de Maistre to make it clear why we should stick with what is long established and not rely on what has been quickly made and is currently fashionable. These writers are part of their times. They are reacting to much turbulence – that is what makes them conservative – but in doing so they put forward enduring arguments which relate to our current times.

These great conservative writers wrote in response to the particular, and were not interested in writing abstract theory in the manner of near contemporaries such as Immanuel Kant and Georg Hegel. Accordingly, we have to pick out the generalities, the nuggets of an enduring social philosophy, from the specifics of their arguments. De Maistre, in his particular opposition to the Enlightenment thinkers, saw himself as an anti-philosophe, of being against philosophy and philosophising as such. He was very much opposed to the late 18th-century attempts to create perfection on earth; he was squarely against any form of utopianism and any refusal to accept human beings as they actually are. As we can see from his famously graphic description of the role of the executioner as the bloody keeper of the social order in his *St Petersburg Dialogues* (1993), he was determined to show human existence in all of its ugliness and apparent cruelty rather than putting forward otherworldly notions of how human civilisation 'ought' to be. De Maistre did not seek to reform or to perfect human society, merely to offer his picture of the world as it actually is.

This anti-theoretical bent, combined with a desire to deal with the present issues, inevitably means that conservative writers tend toward the polemic. As Scruton (2001) states, conservatives tend to favour dogmatics instead of abstract philosophy. This is because they recognise the place of ideology, and do not place their arguments 'outside' of ideology as both Marxists and classical liberals have tended to do. Conservatives believe that we can only go so far with abstractions before we have to face up to things as they are. If we wish to deal with the world we must attempt to see it as it is and not how we feel it should be. This, quite often, is because conservatives are reacting against something specific and concrete rather than arguing for anything that is hypothetical and abstract. What conservatives take as important is what is here now, and not what might be. They naturally enquire how we got to where we are now, and seek to understand this so that they can preserve those elements that are of crucial importance; they wish to hold onto those things which are good and virtuous, which are nourishing of our society and to find the means to preserve them. And they do not treat these things as museum pieces or as anachronisms, but as the forces that motivate and moderate our lives.

We can never attain the perfect state and it is futile and dangerous folly to try: this is the key message from writers such as Burke and de Maistre. We have to accept human beings as they are, and moreover, we can say what they are with confidence: we are not constructed or remade continually out of our social context. We are not, despite what post-structuralists might claim, multiple selves made up of different persona according to a particular social situation; and nor are we made by discourse. Our nature is settled. Of course, part of this nature is to question constantly, to search and to strive for what is new. But if we are honest we know this is because of how we are and how we are able to build on this platform: we search for things as part of what has been passed on to us in a manner that we find accessible and understandable. Unless we have this facility we could not lead a life that is normal and habitual. We could not recognise ourselves for what we are. So for the conservative it is all too obvious that we need a common language and purpose in order to engage in discourse. We could never find our way home without an understanding of where we are going and what we hope to find there when we arrive.

Having said all this we need to question how far politicians, especially of the Conservative variety, actually are concerned with labels. Clearly many contemporary Conservatives wish to be portrayed as progressive, but David Cameron has also referred to himself as a 'liberal Conservative', as well as using the term 'compassionate Conservative' from time to time. Yet he is sufficiently cautious not to be associated too closely with any one thinker or set of ideas. From time to time he has been associated with particular think tanks, for example, Policy Exchange and Res Publica, but he is always clear that he does not directly endorse their agenda or any of their outputs. Cameron, like many politicians, is cautious of becoming too closely associated with any particular label. This lack of concern for labels could not have been shown more clearly than by Cameron's eager acceptance of a coalition in May 2010 with a party that he had spent the previous three weeks of the election campaign criticising. When faced with the only practical means to form a workable government he seized the opportunity and turned a disappointing outcome into a positive result.

But Cameron is not really doing anything dramatically different from what other politicians have done. Tony Blair, before becoming Prime Minister in 1997, associated himself with communitarianism and the ideas of thinkers such as Amitai Etzioni (1993). This helped him to popularise the term 'the Third Way' as an apparently distinctive position in the political centre. He was also heard to use David Selbourne's term 'social-ism' (Selbourne, 1994) as a way of emphasising the communal and the social but without the historical and ideological baggage of traditional socialism. Yet these terms had all been dropped by the start of the second term in 2001 with only 'New Labour' being used, and this had the great virtue of meaning whatever Blair wished it to. Politicians are more concerned with issues and events, and with how they can present themselves in relation to them. So they will use concepts when it suits them, but then quickly drop them if they no longer work, while trying all the while to suggest complete consistency of view.

Tim Bale, in his book *The Conservative party: From Thatcher to Cameron* (2010), argues that successful political parties – that is, those that get elected – are concerned with positioning themselves to match and then meet the aspirations of a plurality of the electorate. Bale's perspective is what he terms 'high politics', where ideology is important but secondary to the play of interests. What matters is the positioning of individuals and parties to ensure they gain and retain sufficient appeal to attain power. Bale argues that the majority of the electorate are at or near the centre, and so this is where a party must position itself if it is to gain power.

Bale certainly has a point, but his definition of politics, based on gaining a plurality at an election, is a rather narrow one. Of course, no politician can achieve anything unless they gain power, but this should not be taken to mean that winning elections is everything. For some their principles are more important than getting elected. They are members or supporters of a particular party because of their beliefs and how this party is seen to represent them. Implementing their ideas is what most people are active in politics for, and so there are clear limits to how far they will be prepared to compromise. Politicians like Cameron and Blair were drawn to particular parties and they did this when they were young, and before they could know of their eventual success as political leaders. So we need to distinguish between the day-to-day of politics on the one hand, and how politicians got into a position of power on the other. At some point they made choices, were motivated and inspired to join one party instead of another, and to choose one faction or another within a party. Cameron may not be a particularly ideological Conservative (Jones, 2008), but he is still a Conservative. This means that, while he will seek to achieve power and so persuade a sufficient number of electors, we should not assume that he would do absolutely anything for it.

But there is a further difficulty with Bale's argument. It is difficult when dealing with the outcome of elections to state accurately the exact constituency for change or reaction. New Labour on three occasions achieved a plurality of support that allowed them a majority in the House of Commons and so to implement their programme. This was accepted as the settled will of the people and commentators could accordingly argue that the country had changed. Political scientists like Bale can seek to measure this by asking voters where they see themselves and the main parties (and their leaders) in terms of a left-right spectrum. In this way it is possible to state how close or distant each party is from the mainstream of opinion (where the mainstream is taken to be close to the centre point of the spectrum). But these positions on the spectrum are averages based on combining the views of all those asked. Consequently most people will fall somewhere either side of the average, and so it does not represent the actual views of all or even many within that plurality.

This has a number of implications. First, it shows that politicians need not gain the support of everyone, or even a majority, particularly in the constituency based first past the post system that has operated in the UK. Blair could claim, and this claim be accepted, that he represented the settled view of the British people, even though a majority voted against him. His view represented the biggest minority, with more people voting against any other single party than Labour. The current government's position is different from this: Cameron's coalition can claim nearly 60% of the electorate as supporters. But many of these voters actively opposed one party to the coalition by voting for the other. The coalition was not what they thought they were voting for when they caste their ballots.

Second, what actually creates the apparent plurality is the very process of gathering the result itself, be it an actual election or an opinion poll. The only way in which the plurality of views becomes manifest is through voters being asked particular questions. These pluralities are not, so to speak, bespoke, but are rather 'off the peg'. Individual voters must accept a total package rather than picking and mixing. Again this means that the reason that a plurality falls apart can be complex and hard to divine. This is also important because it shows how the process shapes the outcome, and accordingly that a different procedure might reach different conclusions. A coalition between the Conservatives and the Liberal Democrats was deemed unlikely and perhaps even unprincipled until the circumstances in May 2010 dictated otherwise. The coalition's majority is legitimate because of the process even if it was, as it were, unconventional and unconsidered prior to the election.

Third, these pluralities are not fixed, but shift, and moreover they do so for different reasons. Some voters will stay loyal to Labour regardless of any event, it being their tribe, while others will move away. They might dislike a particular leader, or feel let down because of a particular policy. As a result, they will fracture off in different directions making it difficult to know what impact the fall in support will have.

For these reasons we can suggest that the representation of a political interest can become self-reinforcing. So, for example, if all major parties seek to claim the progressive label, and these are the only parties capable of forming a government, then the majority are by definition progressive, and reactionaries can be safely ridiculed even though they might be quite as numerous in the electorate.

All this means that reactionaries tend to hide or become reticent to present themselves for what they are. They may be conservatives who feel that the party of that name has left them behind. Alternatively they may believe that they should watch what they say in order to ensure the right result at an election. They might, of course, simply withdraw.

But they would, I wish to suggest, be wrong to do so. This would be to argue that the only parties that are successful are progressive, while unpopular ones are reactionary, with the events in 2001 and 2005 used to vindicate this view. But we can also suggest that some of Thatcher's appeal was her call for a return to so-called 'Victorian values' and a more straightforward and common sense view of the world. Indeed, the most overtly progressive agenda proposed by any party in the last 30 years was that of the Labour party in 1983, with its manifesto subsequently dubbed by one of its own as 'the longest suicide note in history'.

This gloss on progress only works if we accept the almost automatic association of progressive with 'left-wing'. However, Labour in both 1979 and 1983 was not really offering anything new, just a more extensive form of the policies they had tried in the 1970s. The 'change candidate' in both elections was Thatcher. In contrast the leadership of the Labour party seemed from a former generation: they were out of touch and out of date.

Yet, and this is where we start to see the full complexity of this discussion, a lot of Thatcher's rhetoric of change was actually looking backward to a view of Britain with a proud imperial past. But she was able to merge this with a thoroughly modern appeal to personal aspiration and responsibility. What this suggests is that the successful Conservatives are those who are able to merge traditional conservative values with a contemporary programme (one feels that Thatcher might have preferred the term 'radical' instead of progressive). Thatcherism combined the old and the new and for a time it worked.

There is a further point here in relation to Mrs Thatcher's legacy and how she might be viewed. It is interesting that, 20 years after she left office, those who tend to venerate Thatcher most vigorously are now in the traditional wing of the Conservative party. Yet when the Thatcher period began 35 years ago her supporters focused on her economic individualism and radical zeal for change. Partly this is due to a generational shift, in that the Thatcherite young Turks are now elder statesmen. Thatcherism has been assimilated into the mainstream. Indeed, it became the mainstream and there now appears to be no break in continuity. This, of course, is because Thatcherism 'won' the battle of ideas. We might see this as a form of Burkean evolution, of changing to preserve. The Conservative party has been especially good at re-inventing itself, while preserving many of its core ideas and arguments. It has done this intermittently throughout the last 180 years, often in response to splits or electoral defeats (Ramsden, 1998). It has always found the means to restore itself and, along the way, come to terms with changing social, political and economic realities. In other words, it is very good at reacting.

This being so, should we not see Cameron as reacting, and if so what does this tell us about the nature of progress and reaction? Might we not suggest that the formation of a coalition with the apparently left-of-centre Liberal Democrats was actually a supreme piece of reaction? Cameron was faced with a particular set of circumstances and responded accordingly, as indeed did the Liberal Democrats. Seen in this way, of course, reaction loses much of its negative gloss. It becomes a rather more neutral concept, even to the extent of it no longer necessarily being the natural opposite of progress.

The 2010 election has brought forth what has been called a 'new politics', which, the government claims, places the national interest above party interest and sees an apparent move away from the tribal and oppositional forms of politics that has characterised Britain for centuries. Yet just how new is this politics? Is it a radical departure or is it really just more of the same? There have been coalition governments before and these have involved Conservatives and Liberals. Historically this has been one of the main ways that the Conservative party has renewed itself (Ramsden, 1998). In any case, the Conservative party has not shown itself over the last two decades to be a particularly homogeneous and ideologically uniform party (Williams, 1998; Bale, 2010). It too is a coalition of differing views and ideals.

But the Conservative party has always been capable of renewing itself and returning to power, even if it might take time and the decisions taken by its leaders prove controversial (Ramsden, 1998). I shall argue that this has a lot to do with the essentially reactive nature of Conservatism and its ability to respond to changing circumstances. This is an argument that will need some justification, in particular the manner in which I use the term 'reaction' and how it links with notions of tradition and opposition to change.

This book therefore is being written in particular circumstances. Coalitions may not be unknown in the UK, but they are not an expected and normal part of politics in recent times. It therefore is a new situation for those currently active in politics and those writing about it. It is to an extent, therefore, uncharted territory and this means a high degree of uncertainty. The coalition may not last terribly long and so its effects might not be very far reaching. However, it may be that the coalition does create a significant shift in British politics. Whatever is the case, the Cameron government is a coalition and this means that the policies that arise from it may not always be Conservative ones.

Yet, as I have already suggested, Cameron may actually see the link with the Liberal Democrats as enhancing his attempt to pursue a progressive Conservative agenda, and it is these set of circumstances which gives the dichotomy of progress and reaction an additional relevance. What can be seen as a reaction to events has allowed Cameron to develop his agenda in a way he might not have been capable of if he had only a small majority and a much lower share of the vote.

We shall, therefore, take the notion of a new politics at face value and seek to assess its importance. Of course, at the time of writing (October 2010) it is still early days and there are limits to what we can say about the government's policies. But such a study is, I would suggest, of fundamental importance. As we have seen, Cameron has deliberately set out to reshape the Conservative party, a party with a long and illustrious past, but which despite its great electoral successes had fallen on hard times and found itself struggling to re-connect with the electorate. But this attempt to remake the Conservative party is not without its critics. As we shall see, there has been – and continues to be – a debate on the right about the direction of the Conservative party and its acceptance of modernisation. This debate itself can be cast in terms of progress and reaction, between accepting modern Britain as it is and seeking to return to those traditions that are deemed to have served us well in the past.

With the election of David Cameron as Prime Minister in 2010 we are not merely in a post-Brown, or even a post-Blair era, but also a post-Thatcher one, where the current leadership has formed the Conservative party on their own terms and is seeking to make the new government likewise. They have not followed the Thatcherite model, but in a sense, and with due respect, have been operating against it. They are free of the direct influence of Thatcher, not having worked with her, and can see their task as being to some extent one of distancing themselves from it. Of course, her legacy remains, and it is an important one, but there is a sense of moving on, and the formation of the coalition serves only to emphasise this all the more. This too is controversial to those on the right of the party who still revere Baroness Thatcher. However, we might argue that Cameron is merely doing what Thatcher herself did when seeking to move the Conservative party on from the failures of the Heath period (Ramsden, 1998), actions which themselves were not lacking in controversy. Whatever the case, however, it seems appropriate to use this distance between Cameron and Thatcher to compare the approach of each to government as they came to office.

The debate between progress and reaction has perhaps always been at the very heart of Conservatism and is probably irresolvable. It is certainly simplistic, but not entirely unreasonable, to see conservatism in general as a concern for conserving and preserving. But what does this mean in practice when applied a political party seeking to govern? Does preservation mean just doing nothing, of presenting only blind opposition to change? Can conservatism be purely negative, and if it is why should any conservative seek to govern and why create policy?

The critics of Conservatism might indeed seek to portray it in these terms. But why then has Conservatism been so successful in the UK? If it were so relentlessly negative and opposed to everything then why would we expect it to appeal to anyone? Of course, Conservatism has gone a lot further than just saying 'no'. As the Thatcher government shows, Conservatism can be radical and it often promotes considerable and far-reaching change. But does this mean that Thatcherism was not a reaction? Was Thatcher a progressive?

Clearly, therefore, things are rather more complex than simple definitions might suggest. Part of this is the manner in which terms such as progress, reaction and radical are used by politicians and commentators. They are loaded terms and have a history to them, and this means they are used in more complex ways that as a simple dichotomy between good and bad or left and right.

It is a conservative approach that I take in this book, and this, as should now be apparent, consists of a reference back to the past for sources of conservative thinking. Indeed what might be quite surprising to some readers is that much of the debate takes place from, as it were, *within* conservative thought. Much of what I present are debates *between* conservatives and not those of conservatives and their opponents. I take conservative arguments very seriously and do not accept their ready dismissal by the majority of academics. It is not coincidence that the Conservative party has dominated electoral politics in the UK, any more than it was irrelevant that the Labour party found itself electable in 1997 when it accepted much of the Thatcherite legacy. Most academics choose to ignore this fact and do so by only talking to themselves and so perpetuating the illusion that they are part of some consensus. They ignore conservative ideas and so convince themselves that there is nothing serious there. Or worse, they are so certain of their worldview that they assume they know what motivates Conservative politicians without having to engage with what they actually think and do. In both cases the result is a shallow ignorance that refuses to engage with the dominant political ideas of the last century.

In trying to remedy this situation this book deliberately places the coalition's new politics within the context of a detailed discussion of conservatism. Chapters One, Two and Three look at what conservatism is and examine how the concepts of progress and reaction play within this tradition. The discussion then turns in Chapter Four to a consideration of how the Conservatives under Cameron arrived in a coalition government with the Liberal Democrats in 2010. Having done this, the discussion moves backwards in Chapter Five to discover whether this is a new politics. This involves comparing Cameron with the most recent successful Conservative leader, Margaret Thatcher, to determine what differences and similarities there might be. The final chapter makes some concluding remarks about the nature of conservatism and what this can tell us about the Conservative party led by David Cameron. These conclusions are contingent and speculative, but then what can you expect from a conservative?

ONE

The idea of conservatism

Introduction

Conservatives, even those who claim to be progressives, are always keen to associate themselves with a set of traditions and values. The Conservative party led by David Cameron is no different in this regard. The 2010 election manifesto (Conservative Party, 2010a) certainly claimed that the Conservatives under David Cameron's leadership were progressives. However, it also suggested that they were acting in a manner that was entirely consistent with Conservative values and traditions. They were not, the manifesto suggested, breaking with Conservative values, but rather they were bringing them up to date. So, for the Conservatives, being progressive was not anti-conservative, but rather a means of ensuring the continued relevance of tried and tested values.

But what are these values? What are the traditions of Conservatism and in what ways are they compatible with progress? Is there really any merit in claiming to be both 'new' and the 'same old Tories'? This is the question we shall start to answer in this chapter as part of our attempt to understand the nature of conservatism.

Accordingly, much of the discussion in this chapter will be on small 'c' conservatism rather than Conservatism. The latter, of course, relates to the institutions of the British Conservative party, while the former is more general and relates to an ideology that might enclose the Conservatives, but also many other political institutions and ideas. There are many forms of conservatism and so we can expect there to be differences between the British Conservatives and the French Gaullists, German Christian Democrats and US Republicans. However, all forms of conservatism have arisen out of particular circumstance. Conservatism indeed might be seen as the general reaction to circumstance. In the British tradition, the key doctrines and ideas have derived from the reaction to events such as the French Revolution and French imperial expansion in the early 19th century, the opposition to political reform such as the electoral reforms in 1832, the rise of organised labour, Irish Home Rule and relations with the Empire (Ramsden, 1998). In other countries different events have been influential, with the result that conservatism there has evolved in a distinctly different manner. For example, German conservatism was a reaction to the continental dominance of France in the 18th and 19th centuries and the consequent desire to develop a conscious German cultural identity (Watson, 2010). Conservatism is not a bookish ideology, and it is not built on abstract theorising. Rather it depends on events and how politicians, thinkers and people more generally respond to these events.

A disposition

Clearly conservatism is a very pervasive ideology. It appears to exist, in one form or another, wherever there is politics and we can trace the conservative back to the very birth of political ideas. Even if the term was not in use at the time, we can make a case for both Plato and Aristotle being conservative thinkers. But despite its pervasiveness, conservatism is a rather hard ideology to characterise. This is partly because it is primarily an active doctrine that does not lend itself to theorising and so to precise statements: it is a concern for doing rather than thinking.

Conservatism is about what is established, taken for granted and accepted. This does not mean that we resist what is different. Rather it is a concern for how we place ourselves and so understand our position in a large and impersonal world that we know we cannot control. The familiar is therefore a means of coming to terms with our own limits. It is where we seek to hold on to what is close, to what we have got, to what we know as a means of reassuring ourselves and keeping ourselves calm. It allows us to remain located, to be placed rather than displaced, to be home. Where there are many things that we cannot control we seek out and treasure those things we can control. When we feel in danger of being overwhelmed, we seek to blanket ourselves in what we know, what is close to us. The more we fear the unknown the more we depend on what is close.

Most writers on conservatism do not see it as a theory of society but as a disposition. It is a way of thinking and acting which predisposes us towards certain responses. Hence Russell Kirk (1986) can talk of 'The conservative mind', rather than a set of theories or a description of a particular utopia. Fundamentally, conservatives like Kirk believe they are merely recognising and responding to how human beings are. Anthony Giddens (1994) argues that in some circumstances and on some occasions even supposed radicals can show the desire to preserve and conserve, especially when they feel threatened and see the need to protect what they value. Giddens points to certain groups on the left, such as trade unionists and environmentalists who feel that what they hold dear is threatened and so they campaign not for radical change but for preservation. Hence Giddens is able to suggest that there is a rather general disposition which he terms 'philosophical conservatism', and which need have nothing to do with conservatism in a political sense.

But we still have not done any more than hint at what conservatism consists of: we need to be more specific. The problem in doing this though lies precisely in the fact that conservatism is not a set of doctrines. Indeed, as Roger Scruton (2001) argues, it is seldom explicitly articulated by its adherents. He suggests that at one level we should not expect advocates of moderation or a 'middle way' to feel the need to articulate their views. Advocates of 'keeping things as there are' would quite naturally find themselves at a loss to explain why things should be this way. The adherents of conservatism, seen as a general complacency with how things are and the concomitant reluctance to contemplate a movement away from the status quo, would find their position a self-evident one. Scruton states that conservatism 'is characteristically inarticulate, unwilling (and indeed usually unable) to translate itself into formulae or maxims, loath to state its purpose or declare its view' (p 9).

This does not mean that we should not try to define conservatism, or that others have not tried to do so. The simplest definition would be to suggest that conservatives seek to conserve: they aim to keep things as they are. But, quite rightly, Scruton feels that to state that conservatives have a desire to conserve is a rather limp definition. Unlike Giddens' notion of philosophical conservatism, which is described as a general attempt to resist unwelcome change, what needs to be considered is what is to be conserved and why (O'Hara, 2005). It is not enough simply to say that we wish to conserve. We must qualify this by stating what we wish to maintain and why it is so important for us to do so.

What we are aiming to conserve are those things close to us and which we hold dear. So, for Scruton, 'conservatism arises indirectly from the sense that one belongs to some continuing, and pre-existing social order, and that this fact is all-important in determining what to do' (2001, p 10). We feel ourselves to be part of some larger whole, which defines us as individuals. This social entity becomes mingled with the private lives of its members: 'They may feel in themselves the persistence of the will that surrounds them. The conservative instinct is founded in that feeling: it is the enactment of historical vitality, the individual's sense of the society's will to live' (Scruton, 2001, p 10). Expressed in this manner we can see why it might be unarticulated. Scruton sees it almost as a gut reaction, as something elemental. Conservatism is about the relationship we have with those things around us, and in particular here with those social entities that form us and which we therefore identify with as defining our sense of self. As we can see, there is more than a hint of Hegelian idealism in this most English of conservatives (Dooley, 2009). Scruton's connection between individual and social life appears to owe much to Hegel's conception of freedom as consecrated in the bond between individual and society, where we are only free to act because we are located within a social whole (Hegel, 1991).

We can see that conservatives do not necessarily subscribe to individualistic views of the world: individuals are defined in relation to something else, rather than the liberal view whereby individuals are complete in themselves and where their qualities come, as it were, from within. Conservatives believe that we cannot be free unless we are surrounded by some set of social relations that allow us to operate. Conservatives look to things outside of themselves to define them as individuals: they are not sufficient unto themselves, but rely on social institutions and collective notions to sustain them. There is, most conservatives would say, definitely such a thing as society. Scruton sees the conservative instinct deriving from a need to feel connected to some pre-existing social order, and from a need to protect this sense of belonging. We can portray this sense of belonging as a series of concentric circles, which, as it were, ripple out from the self and connect with others. Our initial contact is within the home and in the locality. As Edmund Burke states in one of his most famous remarks: 'To be attached to the subdivision, to love the little platoon we belong to in society, is the first principle (the germ as it were) of public affections. It is the first link in the series by which we proceed towards a love to our country and to mankind' (1999b, pp 136–7). As we shall see in Chapter Five, this notion of 'the little platoons' is referred to explicitly in the 2010 Conservative manifesto as a key reference between long-standing conservative attitudes and the particular form of Conservatism expressed by Cameron and the party he leads.

According to Burke's view, our main contacts are local, but these do not contain our affections, which develop outwards to a love of country and to humanity as a whole. However, this sense of connectedness is not abstract – it is not a concern for human rights or any such abstraction – but based on our concrete relations with people close to us. It is through this connection that we develop our sentiments towards others.

This gives us something of a start in defining conservatism: it is a concern for what is pre-existing and what provides continuity. But we have still only touched the surface, and we need to go deeper. Helpfully for us, Quinton (1993) has pointed to three central elements in conservative thought: traditionalism, scepticism and organicism. These elements are all connected to this sense of continuity, but also inform us as to when and why change might be necessary and acceptable, and how it should be attempted.

Tradition

This first element relates most directly to the view that conservatism is about 'conserving' and reacting to change. Quinton suggests that traditionalism is based on a support for continuity in politics, for the maintenance of existing institutions and practices, and a suspicion of change. Where change is seen as necessary, it should be gradual and only undertaken after careful consideration: it should be evolutionary and piecemeal rather than fundamental and transforming. The ideal for a conservative would be a situation where change comes only in response to extra-political circumstances such as population changes. The political arrangements of a community are, for the conservative, settled and permanent. According to this view, there is little prospect of a coherent progressive conservatism.

But the support for traditionalism does not derive merely from reactionary instincts or inertia (although this may well be present), but from the instrumental effects of these longstanding practices and institutions. It is presumed that these would not have existed for so long without providing some considerable benefit to our ancestors and ourselves. Accordingly, Kekes (1998) identifies a conservative traditionalism that protects those institutions that allow individual autonomy to flourish. This tradition implies the limiting of government's authority to interfere with these institutions. He sees a predisposition to institutional arrangements that promote individual autonomy and that the conservation of tradition serves to embed this sense of liberty. One such institution, of course, is private property rights, but we might also point to the rule of law and the mechanisms that ensure its enforcement.

Perhaps the most famous and elegant discussion of the virtue of tradition is again that of Edmund Burke (1999b), who stated that society is a partnership between the living, the dead and those yet to be born. A society is based on inherited patterns and traditions and the living have a duty to respect the interests of the dead and the unborn. This is because these patterns and traditions embody the interests of the dead and offer a prospectus to the unborn. One respects the dead by preserving and passing on what they have created to those yet to come. Thus social institutions are not ours, but held in trust for future generations. This statement by Burke is also important in its realisation of the organic nature of a society, a doctrine we shall consider below.

For Burke our connection to others is not contractual but is transcendent. The members of society have not come together to form some social contract and there is no sense of consent in our participation in society. A social contract implies that there was something before society, which may have been nasty, brutish and short, but also that individuals can withdraw from their contractual obligations: if we offer our consent, we can also withdraw it. But for Burke there can never be a pre-social existence. Instead some form of society is presupposed in the thinking and acting human actor integrating with others. As Joseph de Maistre (1996) has argued in his critique of Rosseau's philosophy, the very idea of a social contract is illogical. Why would individuals come together to form a contract unless they were convinced that they could trust others and that their commitments would be honoured? Yet, what would a social contract be for if it is not to create trust and enforce relations? The required outcomes of a social contract would therefore already have to exist in order for individuals to come together to form that contract (O'Hear, 1999; Scruton, 2001).

Kirk (1986) presents one of the most concise definitions of the traditional conservative position. He states that 'conservatives inherit from Burke a talent for re-expressing their convictions to fit the time. As a working premise, nevertheless, one can observe here that the essence of social conservatism is preservation of the ancient moral traditions of humanity. Conservatives respect the wisdom of their ancestors' (p 8). Kirk suggests that conservatives 'think society is a spiritual reality, possessing an eternal life but a delicate constitution: it cannot be scrapped and recast as if it were a machine' (p 8). Society is something that is always there, and has a transcendent quality. But this does not mean that it is hardy and capable of rough treatment.

Developing from this Kirk presents what he calls 'six canons of conservative thought' (p 8). First, there is a 'Belief in a transcendent order, or body of natural law, which rules society as well as conscience. Political problems, at bottom, are religious and moral problems' (p 8). Second, he points to an 'Affection for the proliferating variety and mystery of human existence, as opposed to the narrowing uniformity, egalitarianism, and utilitarian aims of most radical systems' (p 8). Third, Kirk points to the 'Conviction that civilised society requires orders and classes, as against the notion of a "classless society"' (p 8). He goes on: 'Ultimate equality in the judgement of God, and equality before courts of law, are recognised by conservatives; but equality of condition, they think, means equality in servitude and boredom' (pp 8–9).

Fourth, Kirk states that conservatives are of the 'Persuasion that freedom and property are closely linked' (p 9) and that 'Economic levelling, they maintain, is not economic progress' (p 9). So conservatives see the importance of property rights and that equality does not equate with progress. Fifth, he points to the importance of prescription and a distrust of abstract design: 'Custom, convention, and old prescription are checks both upon man's anarchic impulse and upon the innovator's lust for power' (p 9). The final canon involves a:

> Recognition that change may not be salutary reform: hasty innovation may be a devouring conflagration, rather than a torch of progress. Society must alter, for prudent change is the means of social preservation; but a statesman must take Providence into his calculations, and a statesman's chief virtue, according to Plato and Burke, is prudence. (p 9)

Kirk, therefore, sees conservatism in religious terms, and in doing so stresses the importance of order, property and prudence.

In justifying traditionalism Quinton offers a number of arguments used by conservatives. First, they cite the effects of unintended consequences, those outcomes of political action that were not, and could not, have been predicted by the actors involved. Changes in one part of the political realm may have consequences that were unforeseen and indeed ripple out to the extent that the repercussions may go considerably beyond the political realm. Of course, unintended consequences need not necessarily be negative – unforeseen change can have positive results. However, it is the sheer unpredictability of change that causes concern for conservatives. If we are unable to predict outcomes with any certainty, how can we rationally propose change? The issue is merely compounded by the fact that the current situation is known – we are aware of what existing institutions offer us, with all their imperfections – whereas the future is always hypothetical. Those with a utopian cast of mind would, of course, see the opposite possibility here, where the future is untainted by the ugly, imperfect present, but for a conservative this is mere wishful thinking. The conservative disposition is very much tied to the present, and if it is looking anywhere it is backwards. So where change is seen as necessary, it should be planned and gradual to ensure that any unplanned effects can be understood and, where necessary (and possible), countermanded. According to Scruton, in order to minimise the dangers involved, change should be continuous and gradual. So conservatism does not mean a rejection of change: 'The desire to conserve is compatible with

all manner of change, provided only that change is also continuity'
(Scruton, 2001, p 11).

This fear of the unexpected is compounded by a second justification
for tradition, which we have already referred to in the introduction as
the 'tightrope approach' to politics. This is the essentially pessimistic
position that there are many ways in which change can go wrong, but
only very few ways of getting it right. Decision makers are balancing
on a very fine line indeed, and the spaces either side are cavernous and
dangerous. This attitude leads to two consequences. The first is that if
change is so difficult and potentially dangerous, we should take great
care in how we undertake it. We should make sure we are properly
prepared (the rope is securely attached, we have the right equipment,
and the weather conditions are not adverse). Second, we should
leave the crossing of tightropes to the experts (Oakeshott, 1962). The
difficulties involved are such that we should not expect all to be able
to manage it. Indeed only very few will have the talents, skills and
experience to get from one side to the other intact. Governing is not
easy, and not only should it be done unencumbered by ideology, but
also only undertaken by those who properly understand what they are
doing. This might not sit easy with modern notions of democracy, but
the conservative would argue that their point is empirical and not based
on any particular call for a return to aristocratic or oligarchic rule. In
any case, the 'tightrope approach' is compatible with democracy, but
not necessarily with all notions of progress and activism in government.
This approach, based as it is on empirical evidence, suggests that not
all traditionalists would concur with Kirk's transcendent approach to
conservatism.

The third justification is also empirical, in that conservatives can
point to many historical examples of bad changes, which have led
to political upheaval, mass murder and even genocide. Since Burke's
time in the late 18th century, conservatives have warned against the
effect of utopian adventure in politics. From the conservative point
of view, there have been far too many examples of bad changes to
make anything acceptable other than changes which are piecemeal,
controlled and evolutionary. This element of traditionalism links into
another key doctrine associated with conservatism, namely a sceptical
view of political knowledge.

But before looking at this second doctrine, I wish to consider
the main criticism of traditionalism. Critics argue that the problem
with traditionalism is that it opposed things that we now all accept,
for example, universal suffrage. Friedrich Hayek, in his famous essay
'Why I am not a Conservative' (postscript to Hayek, 1960), contends

that there is some inconsistency and incoherence in this traditionalist strand of conservatism. Traditional conservatism, according to Hayek, is inconsistent in that is seeks to prevent further change, but not past change that has created the current political settlement which conservatives now support. Universal suffrage is now accepted, but changes brought in by New Labour since 1997 such as the abolition of hereditary peers and the introduction of regional government are opposed for breaking long-standing traditional and local ties. Hayek sees that the problem is to suggest that dynamic societies should stop at some point, which is to the liking of conservative thinkers. Of course, what this leads to is a succession of conservatives saying 'this much and no more'. But in previous generations conservatives opposed what their successors now accept: neither Burke nor de Maistre could be called supporters of mass democracy. Modern conservatives accept democracy and popular sovereignty as a matter of course, but both Burke and de Maistre found this notion thoroughly dangerous. Thus conservatism is seen as incoherent in that it deals with social change differently depending on when it occurred: past change is (now) good, but any further change is bad.

Quinton, however, argues that there is no real inconsistency here, as the high social costs of these changes have now been paid. The costs paid in shifting from aristocracy to democracy have now been covered (and Burke was certainly correct in his predictions of the great human costs of revolution against aristocracy). We therefore quite rationally see the past, which is settled, as different from the future, which is still to be made. Also the social costs of change might well have been lighter if the conservative's call for gradual change had been listened to at the time. But, in any case, these things are now part of the customary established political order and have to be accepted as such. This response by Quinton is pragmatic and practical, but does not deal with Hayek's objection that conservatism is illogical, in that these changes, which conservatives now accept, would never have come about if they had been listened to at the time.

This problem is recognised, in part at least, by Roger Scruton in his book *England: An Elegy* (2000), and it is the subtitle of the book that is important here. Scruton looks back to an ideal of England in the 1950s and before, which he sees as breaking down under the weight of social reform, the Americanisation of popular culture and European integration. But he is also aware that it is neither possible nor necessarily desirable to turn the clock back to this apparent golden age. Change is often only a one-way process, and we cannot undo what has been done and unlearn what we now know. Therefore, for

Scruton, one function for the conservative is to elegise, to remind their fellow citizens of their inheritance and what it means in the here and now. Indeed conservatives must make others aware that the 'here and now' is built on certain foundations and there are consequences to altering those foundations without proper thought. The 'here and now' comes with the heavy baggage which we call the past. The role of the conservative is to put a restraint on change in order to ensure that it is properly thought through and is consistent with the traditions and customs which have developed over time. As Scruton argues, change is acceptable so long as it is also continuity.

With Hayek's comments and the conservative response in mind, we can question more generally just how far conservatism and certain forms of liberalism are compatible. Clearly, the free market emphasis of Thatcherism was derived from classical liberal ideas, with Hayek's thought featuring as an important element. However, as we have seen, Hayek was determined to distance himself from conservatism.

Indeed there are clear differences between these ideologies, particularly relating to attitudes towards authority and autonomy, to duty and liberty, and to order and freedom. But there are overlaps in practice between certain forms of conservatism and liberalism. This might be due to the way in which political parties have developed: as the Liberals declined while also becoming more radical and statist in the early 20th century, the Conservative party took over much of the baggage of classical liberalism and accepted markets and a free economy, individual freedom, personal responsibility and the importance of property ownership. Some of these ideas, such as property and personal responsibility, have always been intrinsic to conservative thought since Burke, but the support for markets is not something the party of King and Country would necessarily have favoured 150 years ago.

Of course, not all conservatives accept the centrality of markets and economic freedom. Many traditional conservatives have been concerned over the destructive nature of liberal policies, as have the so-called 'red Tories', who are critical of the role of the state as well as of laissez-faire economics (Blond, 2010). Traditional conservatives see laissez-faire as being destructive of treasured institutions, particularly those of the community and the family, and again this view is shared by red Tories. Both sets of thinkers oppose individualism with what might be described as a form of conservative communitarianism. They contend that individualism has created a climate of permissiveness and license that threatens family life and local and national loyalties to traditional hierarchies and established forms of behaviour. This is replaced with a 'foreign' culture of American or Australian media and television with an emphasis on the low brow and the cult of celebrity.

Roger Scruton (2001) has argued that conservatism is not necessarily accepting of capitalism. In the 18th and 19th centuries the Tories were the anti-capitalist party, favouring agriculture, traditional hierarchies and aristocratic forms of governance. Free markets and personal freedom might have a utility for many conservatives, in that they are more likely to engender and protect the right sorts of institutions such as the family and private property rights (Kekes, 1998). They allow these institutions to flourish free from interference. However, it has to be stated that no particular form of economic organisation is essential to conservatism.

Conservatives tend to be more pragmatic and less demanding of theoretical purity in their politics. We can see this with the example of Robert Nozick who was briefly courted by the Reagan administration in the early 1980s (Schmidtz, 2002). They were attracted to Nozick's libertarian arguments for the ultra-minimal state and views that taxation was forced labour. However, they quickly dropped him when they came to understand that his brand of libertarianism extended to sexual freedom, the abolition of immigration controls and the legalisation of all drugs. Nozick was far too rigorous and consistent in his libertarianism for any politician to accept wholesale. Politicians tend not to want to accept the totality of a theoretical platform but to pick and choose, to use influential thinkers when they suit their purpose but to remain somewhat distant in case they become tainted with unpopular and impractical ideas. Politicians might state otherwise, but they do not necessarily seek rigour and consistency in their politics.

One key difference between conservatives and liberals is the concept of perfectibility. We shall discuss this idea again when we consider progress in the next chapter, but this is essentially the idea that we can progress towards a better form of society based on clear principles. It may not mean that perfection can ever be achieved, but there is a clear belief, driven by post-Enlightenment liberal thought, that humans and the societies to which they belong can be improved and life made better for all. Libertarians will tend to subscribe to this position and see a particular form of social organisation as being legitimate and morally desirable. Other forms of society are less desirable and morally deficient and so the work of the libertarian is to create the ideal form of society based on the correct principles. However, the conservative has no such plan. They do not accept perfectibility: human beings are not perfectible, but are sinful creatures tainted by their imperfect nature. Therefore conservatives see that we have no alternative but to accept the world as it is. We have no choice but to use what we currently have. We cannot remake the world or wish it away and replace it with something else. The world as it now exists is all that there is, and attempts to create a 'better' world are fraught with dangers as proved by the Terror of 1793 and the history of communism.

Conservatives do not see that any society has a particular end. It is rather an end in itself. There is no other purpose than to maintain society as it is now. It is not legitimate to sacrifice the interests of those living now for those yet to come in the future: trading actual human beings with interests and aspirations of their own for a vague notion of 'the people'. This is tantamount to a situation where a state is actually at war with its citizens, being prepared to use them for utopian ends which may not fit with the actual current interests of its citizens. But society cannot be arbitrarily changed to meet one particular set of purposes. So the world should be accepted as it is, with the interests and aspirations of individuals, and the institutions that underpin them, seen as legitimate and worthwhile in their own right.

When asked what society is for, a conservative might well say it is for what exists for itself. But society encloses not just the living, but also the heritage and the aspirations of that society. It therefore includes the dead, who have created our world and have passed it on to us for us to maintain and add to. It has been entrusted to us by them, and so their interest does not diminish. Society also encloses the unborn, who will inherit what we leave behind and for whom we have a duty to preserve the world as best we can so that they can flourish and prosper.

So looking after what we have now maintains what we have inherited from our ancestors and what we promise to hand on to our successors. Protecting what is 'now' means we retain what was 'then', so that this remains with us 'now', and which we can then use to help preserve 'the future' as a sustainable place. This says little about any particular form of social arrangement or organisation, but allows for traditions to be maintained and for change to occur as a means for preserving these traditions. Government, for a conservative, is a form of maintenance rather than a progression. It is not about creation or building, be it the new Jerusalem or anything else, but of keeping things going.

Scepticism

The second key element of conservatism identified by Quinton (1993) is scepticism about political knowledge. This arises out of the traditional worldview and colours the conservative attitude to social change. Quinton argues:

> Political wisdom ... is embodied ... in the inherited fabric
> of established laws and institutions. This is seen as the deposit
> of a great historical accumulation of small adjustments to
> the political order made by experienced practitioners, acting
> under the pressure of a clearly recognised need in a cautious,
> prudent way. (1993, p 245)

Political wisdom is the accrual of very many tiny adjustments in the political realm. Politicians are seen as operating under the pressure of events, using their accumulated judgements to minimise the adverse consequences of these pressures, and to protect the essential elements within the political fabric. Politics is seen as being a responsive and defensive activity rather than being programmatic.

A sceptical attitude is seen as necessary because there are clear limits to what we can know about the political realm. Kekes (1998) suggests that conservatives are sceptical because, while they might seek to base political arrangements on a rational basis, they recognise that there are distinct limits to reason. Conservatives, according to Kekes, do not reject rationality in political discourse. However, they do see it as limited and by no means a sufficient condition. There are limits to what can be planned for rationally due to the inevitability of unintended consequences. Furthermore, conservatives point to the often bitter consequences of attempts at rational planning, or what might be seen less positively as social engineering. Conservatives are critical of mass social house building and town planning for the same reason (Scruton, 2000).

This critique of rationality and its limitations is most closely associated with Michael Oakeshott and his seminal essay *Rationalism in Politics* (1962). Oakeshott can be seen as an evolutionary conservative. He sees change as inevitable, but where it is necessary it should still be cautious. This is because the consequences of political action are unpredictable: rational planning is prone to failure, if not disaster. Like Kekes, Oakeshott suggests that the purpose of social and civic institutions is to protect our traditional liberties, and these institutions might have to evolve so that these liberties can be preserved. If we are faced with new threats, be they due to globalisation, environmental pollution, demographic change or whatever, those institutions that protect the integrity of a society need to evolve to meet these new threats. Oakeshott is explicit on this evolutionary character, stressing that we develop social institutions out of practice rather than by design and planning. He is fundamentally opposed to rational planning as it demonstrates a misunderstanding of the operation of human experience. His epistemological ideas have a resonance here not only with the libertarian social philosophy of Hayek (1960, 1988) and Mises (1981), but also the epistemology of Heidegger (1962) and Wittgenstein (1953). Like these other thinkers, Oakeshott's critique is epistemological, in that it calls into question what we can know, and, more importantly, what we need to know for us to be members of a viable polity. One gains knowledge of the world, and moves through it, by action and not through rationalisation. This scepticism about human knowledge leads Oakeshott to see politics as a practice that is best performed by those experienced in governing.

There is a further strand to Oakeshott's thinking that is important here, and this is his belief in the need to have a clear relationship between state and citizen. Like some libertarian thinkers, and particularly Hayek, Oakeshott argued that the role of intermediate institutions such as trade unions, the professions and local government need to be tightly constrained to ensure that the proper relationship between state and citizen can be fostered and maintained (Devigne, 1994). This point is developed by Scruton (2001) who sees the relationship between state and citizen (or subject, as he would have it according to the British constitutional tradition) as similar to that of parent and child with the consequent reciprocity of fealty, submission and protection that goes with that relationship. It follows from this that institutions that insinuate themselves between the state and citizen are potentially disruptive to this relationship, bringing with them special and particular interests and grievances that might subvert the direct relation between citizens and their protector.

Scruton suggests, along with Oakeshott, that conservatives do not see any purpose in politics other than governing. We indulge in many activities as ends in themselves, and without any larger purpose. We go fishing, read books, watch films and have relationships with others. These activities are not derivative of anything, nor are they subservient to something else. They are sufficient in themselves as ends. Likewise, as Scruton suggests, a society is already an end: 'Its history, institutions and culture are the repositories of human values' (2001, p 13). Society is not the means to achieve some future goal, but a worthy end in itself as it is now. Individuals have interests, needs and ends now, and there is no reason why these should be sublimated to some future ends that may or may not be realised. Hence Scruton suggests that communism is absurd: individuals are prevented from doing what they may wish to do now, in order to prepare 'the people' – the undivided collective – for some future utopian state in which the ends of others are imposed.

For Scruton there are two axiomatic principles of conservative thinking. First, unlike liberalism and socialism, there is no general politics of conservatism, but it is as varied as the forms of social order. Scruton suggests, that for conservatives, there is 'no purpose beyond that of government' (p 14). He admits that this puts them at a serious disadvantage in relation to socialists: 'they lack any offering with which to stir up the enthusiasm of the crowd. They are concerned solely with the task of government, and their attitude defies translation into a shopping list of social goals' (p 15). In short, all they can offer is a quiet life.

Second, conservatism engages with the surface of things, with the motives, reasons, traditions and values of the society from which it draws its life. Conservatives do not accept that there is a 'hidden reality' that is masked by the ideology of the dominant forces in society, and which can only be laid bare by the work of intellectuals. Rather, for Scruton, the world is precisely as we see it. It is not hidden behind some social construction or hegemonic discourse which serves the end of a particular class. Rather the surface is all there is, with nothing below. This means that attempts to 'discover' the 'true' nature of society and the 'real' interests of humanity are utopian delusions based on an artificial abstraction rather than the world as it actually is. Accordingly, it is illegitimate for anyone to seek to 'remake' the world according to some abstract prescription of what human nature ought to be.

So this sceptical view opposes ends in politics. There are some activities such as friendship and fly-fishing that are pursued for their own ends. These practices depend on skill, and these skills require practice and not the application of book-based theory. We learn how to do many things by practising them, through emulation and by watching those who are already masters in that skill. But we cannot become proficient by book learning or though classroom instruction. Oakeshott believes that governing is just such a skill: it comes through experience and through practice. As Quinton (1993) comments, 'The conservative response to novelty must be a matter of judgement, based on experience, not a business of the application of a set of rigid principles.' (p 261). One cannot pre-empt political action, merely react to it.

But there is also a second reason for a sceptical approach in politics. Conservatives argue that political ends are almost infinitely contestable, and we cannot agree what the 'correct' ends are. The ends of individuals and groups are contestable and plural, with no one set necessarily supplanting all others. There is no mechanism to adjudicate between different notions of the good life. It follows therefore that pursuing one end will impact negatively on others and undermine their realisation. We cannot put all our efforts into pursuing one end – be it equality, social justice or choice – without it impacting negatively on others.

Quinton, like many conservative thinkers, suggests that there is no necessary set of social and political institutions. Rather, Quinton argues that 'the desirability of such institutions for a conservative is relative to the circumstances of a particular time and place, one in which they are historically established' (1993, p 247). Political institutions derive from local historical conditions, which cannot, and should not, be transplanted from one culture to another. This represents the Burkean view that 'politics is circumstantial, a matter of expediency, the prudent pursuit of the advantage of a particular community' (Quinton, 1993, p 251). Politics, so to speak, is always local.

Kekes (1998) agrees that there may be different traditions, institutions and customs that lead to the good life. There is no single blueprint that is universally applicable and that would inevitably lead to human flourishing. Differing social arrangements have developed within different political and social milieu, and these have a particular instrumentality that might not be transferable to a different situation. Kekes' position, however, is not entirely relativistic. He believes that conservatives will agree that certain attitudes – atomism, for instance – will almost certainly erode any set of traditions and institutions. What he is saying instead is that the desire to conserve will lead to distinct political arrangements and these will depend on particular circumstances. Conservatives see the unplanned and unwritten British Constitution as the paradigm case of this distinctiveness (Kirk, 1986; McCue, 1997; Scruton, 2000).

As we have seen, conservatives have an anti-contractual view of society, in that they believe in non-voluntary duties, allegiances and obligations. Society is not instituted through any social contract, rather human life is definitionally social and therefore there could never have been any state of nature or human existence outside of society. Moreover, the ties that bind one to society are neither optional nor conditional. One has duties that override any individual predisposition.

What goes along with this scepticism about universalism is a pessimism that guards against false hopes and rejects the idea of human perfectibility (Kekes, 1998; Scruton, 2010). Conservatives, being anti-utopians, do not believe that a perfect society is achievable or that evil and misfortune can be eradicated. Conservatives, according to writers like Kekes and Jerry Muller (1997), do not believe in progress, or that all situations are improvable. Muller (1997) identifies a belief in human imperfection and what he terms an epistemological modesty, in that there are limits to human knowledge. He suggests that conservatives place a dependence on institutions 'with their own rules, norms, restraints and sanctions' (p 11). These institutions, however, are by no means transferable. Human beings rely on customary rules based on historical experience rather than the continual reinvention of social rules. Like Burke (1999b), Muller uses the term 'prejudice' without any pejorative connotation, but as a pre-judging of a situation according to our habits, customs and experience. This leads on to further qualities identified by Muller, namely, those of historicism and particularism. These relate back to Quinton's point that there can be no universal politics, only those based on circumstance. This again might suggest it is difficult for a conservative to accept progress as desirable in itself.

There are three key criticisms of this sceptical view of political institutions. First, it may lead to a degree of fatalism and inertia. If we believe that things are as they are because of traditions, and that there are epistemological limits to what can be planned, then we may be tempted to argue that we should not change anything at all. If we cannot see into the future, and if we fear the unforeseen, then we may reject all attempts at change. Hence, it might be argued, politics would ossify, and we support institutions merely because of their longevity and what they remind us of. An example of this is the hereditary principle, which many conservatives still support, but which, we might argue, is not necessary for the proper working of Parliament. But this example – of reforming the House of Lords – offers conservatives a response to this criticism. The Blair government in 1999 reduced the number of hereditary peers and signalled its intention to undertake fundamental reform of the Lords. Yet it had no apparent plan, having carried out what it called 'stage one' reforms without any idea of what 'stage two' might consist of. Over a decade later there was still no clear way forward for how these reforms would be completed. The conservative view would be to argue why it is necessary to change something that works well, in the sense of holding government to account and being a repository of expert opinion which links back to the British political tradition, and to replace it with something as yet unspecified. Conservatives would want to know why these changes are being made, and whether it is not just a case of change for its own sake, of a governing party desperate to appear 'modern' without any proper conception of what modern means and where it leads to.

A second criticism of this sceptical approach is that support for the status quo is merely a disguise for protecting certain vested interests. Conservatism, it is said, is merely an attempt to preserve traditional institutions and liberties, and seeks to maintain the status quo as a position where one class or group dominates. The argument behind the vested interest position is that the majority can be duped, that they are more stupid or gullible than the enlightened minority who are capable of seeing through the deception, the hegemonic discourse, social construction or false consciousness. But to hold this position the enlightened progressive must adhere to a belief in the stupidity and/or venality of the masses. But this seems to run counter to the optimistic vision of the progressive. In order to maintain that conservatism is a vested interest, progressives have to argue that the electorate can be fooled or deceived into voting against their 'objective' class interests. But this is a rather negative and pessimistic view of human capabilities, which, of course, is entirely at odds with their own supposedly optimistic ideology. But how can they expect the electorate to follow the progressive cause if they are so easily led astray? Perhaps what progressives have to do then is to 'force' individuals to act in their own interests. But why should they need forcing if it is in their nature to seek progress? There does, therefore, seem to be something of a contradiction here between what progressives claim and the electorate's apparent susceptibility to deceit at the hands of cruel conservatives. Which would progressives have us believe is true? Honderich (1990), for example, argues that the aim of conservative ideology is only to protect property ownership and existing property relations. Private property rights merely institutionalise existing inequalities. There is thus no particular merit in these institutions if all they do is to entrench property rights that exclude a large number of people.

The response to this position is twofold. First, one way of characterising pluralism is as a series of vested interests which compete and which may not always be reconcilable (Gray, 2009). The conservative position can be seen to an extent as agonistic, in that the multiplicity of interests within a society cannot always be reconciled. But conservatives such as Kekes (1998) would argue that there are some institutions that are better able to accommodate pluralism than others. Such conservatives would argue that the rule of law and the protection of individual freedoms will best guarantee that no single interest supplants another. Having said this, in UK politics only one major party actually identifies itself explicitly with an interest group, and that, of course, is the Labour party.

The second response to the vested interest argument is that it is implausible to suggest that some institutions would have survived, and been maintained in the last century by all parties (including that of organised labour), without them having some utility for all groups. Indeed, it is a matter of fact that all parts of British society have prospered in absolute terms over the last century. What we appear to have, therefore, is a set of institutions in which the party of organised labour can pursue its vested interests without this having overly detrimental effects on other interests.

When discussing whether conservatism is merely a vested interest we are faced with two clear facts. First, Conservatism in the UK has been associated with privilege, aristocracy and property. Since the decline of classical liberalism it too has been the political force most associated with capitalism and business. But, second, the Conservative party's domination of British politics began with the extension of the suffrage and became only stronger the more the country moved towards universal suffrage. It was after the reform acts of 1867 and 1888 that the Conservatives, particularly under the aristocratic Lord Salisbury, became the dominant force in British politics. Indeed, there has always been support from the lower middle classes and upper working classes, which culminated in the long dominance of the Conservatives between 1951 and 1964, and 1979 and 1997. The Conservatives have long enjoyed support from the working class, and could not have been elected into office without it.

As I have suggested, the only major party that actually declares a vested interest through its name is the Labour party, established by the trade unions to pursue their interests and still largely funded by them. Despite Tony Blair's efforts to reform the party and make it independent (Blair, 2010), Labour remains organisationally and financially linked to the trade unions. Alternatively, the Conservative party is defined by a disposition or attitude which could be, and is, held by anyone regardless of income, class or status. It may well be that certain types are more inclined towards conservatism, and this may include the privileged and propertied. But there are two important points to make here. First, many people have a stake in the country and society in which they live and this is not just tied to wealth and property, but relates to shared traditions, language, history and so on. It relates not to income or wealth, but to a sense of ancestry, allegiance and affiliation. Second, the Conservatives have actively sought to increase the numbers of those who share in the system through wider property ownership and through the use of popular democracy as a positive tool of engagement. While all political parties have shrunk in terms of membership, the Conservatives have been and remain the largest in terms of membership. Much Conservative public policy since the start of the 20th century has been conceived not on the basis of maintaining existing privilege but with extending it. They have certainly sought to maintain pre-existing structures and institutions such as the Church, the House of Lords and so on, but they have accepted the reforms of Liberal and Labour governments in terms of welfare provision, education, health and council housing, and have managed these services for a majority of their existence. They might not have introduced many of these reforms, but have not sought to repeal them. So the Conservatives have not indulged in class war. We might say that the country would certainly have been different if election results had been different in, say, 1910 and 1945, but perhaps not as fundamentally as some might think.

While there has always been a traditionalist wing in the Conservative party, which has had greater or lesser impact on issues such as Imperial Preference, defending the privileges of the Lords, opposing the NHS, the abolition of grammar schools and closer links with Europe, the mainstream of the party has largely accepted reform and change and sought to manage it in a way that preserves key institutions and traditions. Perhaps we might see an exception with Mrs Thatcher, who was a determined reformist. Yet she was also the most populist and electorally successful Conservative leader in the 20th century with her policies of privatisation and selling council houses. These policies did not seek to embed privilege, but were precisely the opposite. They watered down privilege by extending property and share ownership to the majority. In addition, her governments attacked vested interests like the professions, monopolists and trade unions. The Thatcher period was actually one of increasing social mobility for the lower middle class and upper working class, a process which only began to stall when New Labour started its policy of feeding the public sector interests from 2001 onwards. But Mrs Thatcher was able to achieve this while maintaining a traditionalist rhetoric.

Where the argument about vested interests is used most often with regard to the Conservatives is over property ownership. Historically the Conservatives have been linked to the landed interest and the aristocracy. They were responsible for the first wave of mass property ownership in the 1930s (Boddy, 1992) and of course they kick-started the shift away from council housing in the 1980s with the Right to Buy (King, 2010a). But this was not seen as being about privilege, but developing a 'property owning democracy', a term coined by Anthony Eden in the 1950s and subsequently developed by Mrs Thatcher to great effect in the 1980s. However, this slogan only took on a meaning and significance because property ownership was within the reach of the majority. It was a clear possibility for them, and so was not merely an enticement on the part of the Conservatives but a legitimation of a now common aspiration. It was rather a case, therefore, of the Conservatives recognising this aspiration and tapping into it. They realised that the heightened affluence and capability within many households needed fulfilling. In this sense, if we are to assume that the move was a calculated one, it could be portrayed as being more expedient rather than protecting a vested interest. In contrast, the party of Labour fought to turn back these aspirations until it became absolutely clear in the mid-1980s that it would lead to their demise as a serious national party. It was only by adopting the same rhetoric of aspiration as the Conservatives that Labour was able to find sufficient trust to be elected again in 1997.

The Conservatives, of course, have not been without their prejudices. They have been, and still are, over-representative of wealth, private education and Oxbridge in the higher echelons of the party (but then the same applies for the Labour and Liberal Democrat leaderships). Yet, as early as the 1860s they elected Benjamin Disraeli, an exotic outsider and son of a convert from Judaism, as leader. They, of course, elected the first female leader in 1975, and indeed between 1964 and 2005 were conspicuously classless in their leaders, with the appointment of a succession of state school graduates. The election of Eton-educated David Cameron was a shift from this classless background, but was perhaps made possible because of the background of the Prime Minister at the time, the Fettes-educated Tony Blair.

One final point we might make is that if the Conservatives do represent a vested interest they did a remarkably bad job in protecting that interest between 1997 and 2010. We might therefore question where this interest has gone and why after four election victories between 1979 and 1992 the Conservatives had proved incapable of retaining power or even gaining much of the ground they lost in 1997. The easiest, and most rational, explanation, of course, is that no such vested interest exists.

A rather more serious criticism of scepticism in politics, particularly the Oakeshottian critique of rationality, is that it clashes most with the experience of really existing Conservatism. Indeed, it is perhaps this particular element of conservative thought that is most at odds with the rhetoric of Conservative politicians seeking to address a progressive agenda. In modern politics we can question whether it remains possible for a politician to admit that he or she has no real sense of direction and furthermore sees no need for one. Ronald Reagan may have said in response to some call for action, 'Don't just do something, stand there!', but he was perhaps the exception (and, indeed, he was not always inactive himself). Politics is now about the presentation of a vision. Mrs Thatcher was not a politician who sat back and awaited events, merely taking them on their merits (or rather she did not present herself as such). Instead, she had a particular vision of where she wished to take Britain.

But beyond this, there is the belief that politicians have an almost universal competence: there is no longer any area of economic, social and cultural life that is beyond politics. When London made its bid to host the Olympic Games, or when it was decided to build a new national football stadium, the government could not resist getting and staying involved. Even the 2000 millennium celebrations were run by a government minister and consequently were directed to meet certain political purposes. There is no real difference between the political parties in this regard: if there is an issue or a problem, politicians are asked to respond and dare not refuse. Current Conservative politicians might say that they want to reduce the role of the state, but this is only at the margins, and in the meantime they have plenty to say on the marketing strategies shops use to sell chocolate.[1]

Yet we might again ask how much of a contradiction there is here. As we have seen, conservatives rest their politics on a sense of tradition and a particularist view of political culture. Thus if circumstances change – and even if these circumstances might not be as conservatives would have wished – then a conservative, to be consistent, must work within these changes and make the best of them. Pragmatically there is no alternative: if the culture evolves, as we would expect it to, then so must politicians. We might suggest it is precisely the realisation of this essentially conservative idea that has led to the electoral successes of the Labour party under Tony Blair. In any case, we should not see conservatives as being anti-government. While the Thatcher period was dominated by market-based economics and a rhetoric of a smaller state, the actual outcome of many of the policies of this period were to increase the role of the state. Indeed, the arguments of thinkers like Scruton (2001) wishing to clear the clutter from the relationship between state and subject imply a strong and paternal state.

Organicism

This brings us to the third doctrine identified by Quinton (1993). This is the belief that human beings and society are organically connected. Human beings are not fully independent of the social institutions and practices within which they grow up. We have seen this already when discussing Scruton's rather Hegelian sense of the conservative instinct. An individual's sense of self depends on his or her appreciation that they are part of a social whole. Moreover, this social whole is specific to time and place. They are not part of 'humanity' as such, nor is it the case that humans need to be part of any community. As we have seen, each individual belongs to their sub-division and their little platoon (Burke, 1999b). For the conservative, what matters is that we feel part of our own community. We cannot, to reiterate, suggest that there is one particular form of social organisation that best fits humanity.

Many people retain an affection for their country, and wish to support it. This may take the form of supporting sporting teams, or perhaps defending it when friends or acquaintances disparage aspects of the country. We might laugh at or be critical of certain things – politicians, the railways, the weather – but do this with exasperation rather than with malice. We feel we have the right to be critical because it is our country, but this is not a liberty we would readily grant to others. In any case, our support for our country will be low key and not involve any great public show. Some of us might get excited during sporting contests or at events like the Last Night of the Proms. Generally, however, the sense of patriotism we have is rather quiet. This does not mean that it is not strong and resilient. And it will generally be stronger among conservatives, for whom a sense of allegiance will appear to be both normal and necessary.

Our affiliation might, however, only be stated negatively, as a sense of disappointment towards the actions of government (especially if it is not a Conservative government), or as scepticism towards the fortunes of our national sports teams, where optimism is always tinged with the fear of imminent defeat as soon as either we face the Germans at football or the Australians at cricket. Shows of patriotism, amongst the English at least (who form the bulk of Conservatives in the UK), are likely to be limited and understated. This may differ for the Scots and Welsh, who may well show their patriotism through a resentment of the English.

But understated or not, for conservatives there remains this sense of patriotism and allegiance. It is based on what is known and what is comfortable, what we are used to. This, we think, is just how things are, and we basically like it this way. A commonplace definition of a conservative might be that they are generally happy with things as they are. Of course, this feeling might be less secure when the conservatives are not in office. In this case, there is perhaps a mild fear of what is, or might, be lost: are institutions under threat, is the country changing too quickly? The conservative will want things to stay the same and is happy when they are. When things do change or are under threat, then conservatives become unhappy and fearful. And if they feel that the Conservative party itself is changing and might not represent their views then they really might start to worry, and with some justification: what is the Conservative party for?

Politics operates within a particular culture and that which exists in the UK might be described as conservative, being based largely on tradition and precedent. The UK has no written constitution and still sees no real need for one. Things only change gradually and slowly, but even when change does occur it is contested and controversial: there are always those for whom any change is too much. This is part of the basic disposition that all politics sits within and which exists regardless of the rhetoric of progress used by politicians. Change may be speeded up or slowed down; people may feel more of less threatened by change, and seek more or less of it, but this change is always conditioned by the prevailing culture and this places an implicit, and sometimes explicit, limit on change. When we hear politicians talking of change we do not believe they seek to change the fundamental institutions of the state. Whatever change occurs, we expect most things to remain intact. Revolution is not, properly speaking, impossible, but it is so unlikely and so unwanted for us here and now that we can effectively outlaw it to the outer fringes of politics. We simply do not feel that so much is wrong with how we live. There may be times when we sense things are not right, and we may show our disapproval, as in the case of MPs' expenses in 2009. But we want things to be sorted out, not the system overthrown. We do not want to start again with a clean state, but rather to return things to how they were when we considered they worked properly. This was when we could safely ignore things and focus on ourselves.

What matters is that our institutions and practices work for us. They may not be perfect and we may have much that we might wish to criticise. These institutions and practices have developed over time, changing incrementally, often unnoticed by many. We can be comfortable with these arrangements and take them for granted. We can accept them because they seem to be accepting of us and of how we are. These arrangements have not been constructed purposefully, or out of some plan, but have developed organically: they have evolved to fit around us. Most of the population, then, can accept a Conservative–Liberal Democrat coalition because it simply does not appear that threatening: what in terms of their everyday life has changed?

Conservatives again rely on empirical evidence in support of their organicist view of community. First, they point to the existence of distinct and separate cultures, which are usually defined by a common language. These cultures also have their own sense of community, culture and belonging. Quinton (1993) goes so far as to suggest that this is indicative of distinct national characteristics. This is a very important part of the conservative view, in that it stresses the deep significance of place and a sense of home as an organising principle for our lives.

The second empirical support is that 'Western' political models, such as liberal democracy and Marxism, have not been particularly exportable to the developing world. Where they have been exported they have often been hybridised by the local political culture and have developed into something that is quite specific to that culture. This, however, raises an interesting point in that the dominant Western political model that has been exported to the developing world since 2000 has been a form of liberal democracy sponsored by so-called 'neo-conservatives'. This would suggest that conservatives have sought to implant a universal model of liberal democracy onto distinctly different cultures such as Afghanistan and Iraq. However, as the leading neo-conservative, Irving Kristol (1995) has acknowledged, the label of 'neo-conservatism' was not chosen but attached by left-wing opponents to try and identify what was a rather perplexing position. Neo-conservatism tends to consist of social conservatism, a hawkish foreign policy, but an activist sense of government which is at peace with the state as the provider of mass welfare services. Indeed, neo-conservatives such as Irving Kristol and his wife, Gertrude Himmelfarb, were Trotskyites in the 1930s, who slowly drifted from the extreme left through the Democratic party to become Republican supporters of Reagan and the second Bush (Kristol, 1995; Heilbrunn, 2008). Heilbrunn (2008) argues that even though the neo-conservatives moved dramatically away from their leftist roots, they did not change their basic attitude towards politics, which was based on direct action and of placing principle over pragmatism. More traditional conservatives, such as Paul Gottfried (2007), have tended to see the neo-conservatives as a take-over of the American conservative movement by former leftists rather than a development out of the bona fide conservative tradition. But whether the neo-conservatives belong to the tradition or not we can still argue that their attempts to grow liberal democracy in Iraq and Afghanistan have been failures, which only further substantiates Quinton's argument that Western models cannot be readily transplanted out of their natural environment.

The idea of organicism can be seen on a number of levels. It can be taken as both a logical and metaphysical necessity, as indeed it is in Hegel's Philosophy of Right (1991). It is the belief in an absolutely necessary connection to a particular community. Scruton goes somewhere towards this Hegelian position, but without losing his English scepticism (Dooley, 2009). Indeed, we need not take such an essentialist position as that of Hegel. Instead a more down-to-earth view would be simply to suggest that individuals are formed within a particular culture and can do little without a connection into social networks. Nevertheless, this view can still be criticised.

First, it can be suggested that this organicist view neglects the fact that individuals are linked into a multiplicity of social relations ranging from family, school, local community, work group, and so on, all of which are likely to be more influential than society as a distinct entity. Individuals may see their primary connection as being to their family or local community rather than to the whole. Yet this is only a problem for the organicist view if we ignore the fact that these other social formations are part of the whole and have been formed within it. It is entirely consistent with the organist view to suggest that individuals might relate to different parts of a complex but ultimately inter-linked whole. These smaller units are really nothing more than Burke's little platoons, which, as we have seen, link to the larger whole.

The second criticism is that precisely because this position suggests that all parts are linked together, it denies innovation. Now this is undeniably true: there are particular ways of doing things and this means that certain approaches should be seen as inappropriate. But what is important here is that, while formally speaking innovation is denied in politics, it is not in any other sphere. Organicism does not deny innovation in the arts or in science or other aspects of cultural life. This simple form of organic relation is not a metaphysical necessity but a matter of political culture. It is a relation between state and citizen and nothing further.

We are now in a position to take stock. We have discussed three ideas – traditionalism, scepticism and organicism – which are central to conservatism. They are clearly connected together and form a unified sense of what conservatism is. I would contend that this view of conservatism is an entirely conventional one. I have not sought to be controversial and to state that a conservative must be of one particular leaning and not another. My aim has been to show that it is possible for a plurality of opinion to exist within conservatism, and that it will naturally evolve and develop as circumstances dictate. Yet there is still something that is identifiable and which will link conservatives across time and place. Conservatism is an idea that cares about the specific over the general. But this means that it can be both open to what is new – to progress – and to what is traditional and so reject the new. What matters are the specific circumstances in which we find ourselves.

On one level this discussion has remained rather distant from the new politics of Cameron's coalition government. It has been a rather general discussion that has not found much to say about events since May 2010. Yet we have started to tease out what conservatism means and this will allow us to connect with the concrete events of politics. In particular, what we are now able to do, having set down a definition of conservatism, is to consider the idea of progress and its opposite – reaction and tradition – and to see what sense we can make of these ideas for modern Conservatism.

Note

[1] Soon after his election as party leader David Cameron criticised the tactic used by some retailers to put chocolate near their tills.

TWO

The lure of progress

Introduction

The political events of 2010 have shown us that it is no longer apparently enough just to be a Conservative; one must now be a progressive Conservative. One must believe in the transformation of society, and to seek fundamental change. Government is there to reform and to create change not just to govern. We might put this down to over a decade of opposition and to continual electoral failure. Moreover, if Labour could get elected in 1997 by seeming to ape Conservative rhetoric, perhaps the reverse might work for the Tories. If the people want progress then why shouldn't we say they can have it? This may, however, be to show too much cynicism and contempt towards politicians.

So let us start by assuming that there is something important in progress and try to work out what is its allure. We need to ask why it is that politicians feel the need to claim they are progressive. Is it simply because everyone else does it? Or is the promise of making things better so irresistible? After all, a better life is what politicians should be in the business of providing for their electorate.

But we have another question to answer: in the light of our description of conservatism, is it really consistent with conservatism to be a progressive and why should David Cameron think that it is? We shall attempt to answer this question in this chapter and the one that follows and we shall do this by considering some aspects of the idea of progress and countering it with the notion of reaction.

Past, present and future

The idea of progress carries with it the notion of perfectibility (Gray, 1993, 2009; O'Hear, 1999). As we have seen, this is the idea that human society and human beings themselves can improve to a higher stage of development, and if not exactly attain the perfect society, then aspire to something near to it. Human beings through their increasing knowledge, greater enlightenment and fuller cooperation can achieve a better society than that which exists today. Perfectibility is to see human societies as developing upwards to higher levels of achievement and development and so leaving behind outdated forms of social organisation, superstition and belief (Oakeshott, 1962). What matters with perfectibility is not that human societies actually attain perfection or indeed anything near to it, but that the attempt to achieve it is worth the effort and that it is quite natural for us to try. It is seen as part of human nature to strive for greater knowledge and understanding and then to apply this understanding to advance human flourishing.

Human history can indeed be seen as a progression in which societies become more complex, where we develop a deeper and fuller understanding of the world around us and are better able to deal with long-standing problems and disasters that periodically face us such as feeding ourselves, living in peace together and controlling our environment. Of course, this statement can be contested: by environmentalists, by those in the developing world, and by those who refuse to see the Holocaust and the Rwandan genocide as aberrations from the upward flow of history. My aim here, however, is not to undertake a full consideration of utopian arguments, but merely to state that this view is a pervasive one and that it sits behind and justifies the clarion call for progress we hear from modern politicians.

Politics, according to this view, is about creating a better society and so it is in the nature of politicians to look to the future and to claim that things will improve. It may be that some sacrifices need to be made in the present, but these are worth bearing for the benefits that will surely accrue in the future. There is an obvious appeal in looking to the future in that we can always claim that things will improve and life will get better without the risk of being proved wrong (at least not yet!). The problem with the present is that it is always known, in all of its shortcomings, its inequalities and disappointments. We can point to what is wrong with how we live now. We have the evidence squarely in front of us on which to base our disappointment. Yet, in contrast, the future is not yet formed. This means that things might get better, that the problems of today can be superseded and a better life had. The future has not yet disappointed us and so it might not. Being unformed it is still full of potential, and importantly it might be possible for us to assist in its forming. We ourselves can help to make a better future; we can have an influence in creating what is not yet made, and so we can make it according to our liking. We do not, then, have to take what we are given, to accept our lot as single atoms in a great universe. We can be in control, we can make a difference, we matter. The future is where we can shine and be as we are intended to be. In the as yet unformed future what is there to stop us?

The present, with its failures, troubles and disappointments, can seem all too real. It is there in front of us, mocking our imperfections. The future, by contrast, can inspire us and let us hope that we can be less troubled, disappointed and that we can be a success. We are prepared to listen to politicians who can so inspire us and lead us to the promised land. Skilled politicians like Tony Blair and Barack Obama are able to persuade people to invest in them on the basis of these promises for the future, and they can do so because many of us want it to be true. By following the lead of these politicians we can leave our dull present with all its failures behind.

But there is a problem: what is now the present was once the future. Tony Blair is now a retired politician and one who led his country in a war based on false assumptions and who most certainly did not eradicate child poverty. So one way of seeing the present is as a past future realised. It is what the potential of the future turned into. The present in which we now live is what those in the past were able to create in all their optimism and desire for perfection. This is what their hopes have amounted to despite their idealism and sincere desire for progress. This present is by no means free from imperfections and many of the desires of its creators remain unfulfilled. They have not made a perfect world; rather it remains a flawed one.

What follows from this is that, if those who came before us could not achieve perfection, why should we now expect to be able to make a better future for ourselves? What is different about us compared to our ancestors that will allow us to succeed where they have failed? Do we really know that much more? Are we really better informed and better prepared? Are we really more enlightened?

Of course, we might think that we are, but then this is precisely what our ancestors felt as well. It is this conceit, that we are an improvement on what came before us, which perfectibility needs to build on. We need to believe that we are building on the progress of the past and that we are now at the highest stage of human development: we simply do know better. Accordingly, we can now plan with confidence, sure in the knowledge that we are better prepared than ever. But this belief in our own rectitude leads us to doubt those who came before us and to question whether they actually knew as much as they thought. Their confidence in their abilities, we might think, was misplaced. On the basis of what we know now we can say that our ancestors were misled, ignorant, bigoted even.

But if they, in the light of later generations, were shown to be mistaken, then again what about us? Why should we be different? Might it not make more sense, in the light of experience, for us to learn that if our ancestors failed in the past, then we may well fail in the future? If the current society in which we live is the fruit of accumulated human actions, successful or not, then why should our efforts prove to be different?

Measuring progress

What often prevents us from falling to this rather glum conclusion is the fact that progress is very seldom defined. It is frequent to hear the term used, but less common to actually gain any sense of what it might mean to progress. Yes, it means that things will change, and that this change is presumed to be for the better, but this does not tell us what our future will look like. While it might seem absurd that we can be sold a vague generality by politicians this is precisely why it works, because it is so vague and general, and so it can mean anything we want it to. We cannot measure progress, and perhaps have no real conception of how we might go about this. On what scale, and over what time period would we judge it, and on whose criteria? Should we judge progress on the basis of the original intentions of those who made them, or according to the judgement of those who are experiencing the outcomes? But it is not unusual for any outcome to be contested. What for one person might appear to be progress would be seen as a backward step by another. For example, is the privatisation of public utilities progress or a regression? Was socialism a step forward or a return to primitive barbarism in which no one was expected to show any personal responsibility for themselves or others? We know that some will say yes to one side of these propositions and others will disagree, but how do we decide who is right and what basis is there for doing so? We might get general agreement on long made changes such as the ending of slavery, universal suffrage, full participation in education, the ending of the death penalty, and so on, but even with some of these the agreement is never total. On other issues, there is no real possibility of consensus.

But when it comes to progress why should we accept a majority decision? For example, why should a simple majority on abortion (by a vote in Parliament made up of elected representatives) bind a minority who find it completely unacceptable on moral and religious grounds? Of course, we might say that they should accept it because it is the law (and this will often be sufficient for a conservative). But this is law created by humans and by deliberation and not through any transcendental process. It is law – and taken as progress – because of a majority vote. In other states, such as Ireland, there is only limited legal abortion and a presumption in favour of the unborn child, presumably because this would be seen as a rejection of long held religious values on the sanctity of human life. But what does this mean for those who disagree with this legal position? May they not have their view? Is it not acceptable to dissent? Does it make it more likely that an opponent will change their view just because they find themselves to be in a minority?

Should we be happy if 51% of a given population claim progress, even if it means that 49% feel worse off? What about if the level of progress felt by 10% – the very poorest, perhaps – outweighs the other 90%? Would we see this as acceptable? Ought we to accept any level of progress if some are still suffering or made worse off as a result? For instance, if the slave states in the USA developed economically (in terms of per capita income for *all* persons in those states) should this be seen as progress even though it was done on the back of an enslaved minority? If progress is a concern for moral and social reform on what basis can we take a simple majority as a guide to progress?

On the other hand, we might see that a moral improvement can only be achieved through sacrifice by the majority through rationing, compulsory unpaid work, conscription into the armed forces or high levels of taxation. All of these might prove unpopular and be disliked by a considerable number such that they would need to be enforced by a degree of coercion. In some socialist societies governments have asked – or rather demanded – that the people make sacrifices for the future well-being of that society. Likewise, a perceived moral improvement in a society might need the imposition of chastity or abstinence and the prohibition of certain behaviours in particular parts of the population (the young and unmarried, for instance). These sacrifices and prohibitions might need to remain for a lengthy time frame in order for their benefit to society to be realised, such that many citizens may not actually experience the benefit of progress for a considerable time or even at all. Some may effectively be called upon to sacrifice their well-being for the good of future generations. But why should we see this as progress? Why should we see it as an improvement if many people die or lead poor quality lives so that an indeterminate number of people can lead a better life at some as yet unspecified time in the future? What makes future benefits better than those that might accrue in the present?

John Gray (1993) has argued that conservatives have sound reasons to reject the idea of progress. He argues that we lack the means to measure progress and improvement in human affairs. But he goes further than this. Gray argues that 'the idea of progress is particularly pernicious when it acts to suppress awareness of mystery and tragedy in human life' (p 138). He feels that peddling the idea that life will be better in the future, and that sacrifices and suffering by people today are therefore worthwhile, 'corrupts our perception of human life, in which the fate of each individual is – for him or her – an ultimate fact, which no improvement in the life of the species can alter or redeem' (p 139). We are, so to speak, equal under God and so no one life can be used for the purpose of furthering the project of another.

Gray also suggests that 'the project of universal improvement' (p 139) can be questioned in that 'the eradication of one evil typically spawns others, and many goods are dependent for their existence on evils' (p 139). In other words we cannot know what effect our efforts at improvement might have and whether they will actually make our lives better or worse. Gray also agrees with anti-enlightenment thinkers such as Herder, who question the commensurability of human goods and so argue it is incoherent to talk about making progress. In other words, if there is no such things as a universal good, that applies to all cultures, how can we state that progress is being, or even can be, made?

Lastly, Gray sees progress as a 'surrogate for spiritual meaning' (p 139), which encourages us to see our lives 'not under the aspect of eternity, but as moments in a universal process of betterment' (p 139). Instead of living for now and accepting our place in the world and our life as it is, we instead are always looking forward to what we might become. Gray argues that 'the idea of progress reinforces the restless discontent that is one of the diseases of modernity' (p 139). We are never content with our lot, but instead are constantly striving for that which is always just beyond us.

An important question that flows from this critique is just who does the measuring of the progress achieved? Moral improvement will often be judged by the very ones who advocated the improvement. In order to push forward change they need power to impose their will and will most likely remain of considerable influence afterwards and so be able to determine success. Those who initiate progress are presumed to be the ones best able to measure it. And because they retain their influence over others, they are also able to deal with dissent and criticism of their view of progress. They can claim that this opposition is ignorant and needs to be reformed and 're-educated' so that they can appreciate the benefits of change: it is, after all, for their own good for dissenters to be improved along with everyone else. As Isaiah Berlin (1969) has suggested, those who refute progress can readily be seen to be perverse and seeking to hold back humanity (including themselves) and therefore it is entirely legitimate for those who understand humanity's true nature to remedy these personal faults by the appropriate action. Dissenting from the approved path of progress for the Soviet people was an expression of mental illness and needed the appropriate treatment. To have the power to determine what is progress and when it has been achieved is to be able to exert considerable control over the lives of people.

The perception of progress

However, the call for progress need not be so devastating and in democracies the effect is often more benign. What matters for democratic politicians and their audience alike is that to call for progress is to make a claim of optimism. We can state that our prospects will improve and that our potential can be fully tapped. The lure of progress is precisely that it is optimistic. It provides us with the promise of something better. Progress, as banal as it sounds, is simply about making peoples' lives better.

What does not seem to matter is that, in practice, progress is seldom actually achieved. The reason for this is that politicians have no real interest in defining or in limiting progress. They do not say how progress is to be measured and what is to count as success, and nor do they admit to the near impossibility of doing so. Instead they tend to remain vague and rely on statements that 'things can only get better', as New Labour's 1997 election song told us. But New Labour did not provide us with the details of how this would be proved or measured and how they should be held to account. Indeed the whole point of the declaration of progress was not that certain outcomes would so derive, but rather the message it sent out. Indeed a progressive politician need not actually make any progress. All they need do, as New Labour certainly succeeded in doing, is to appropriate the label and prevent others from using it. The battle is to ensure that the label 'progress' can be stuck to them and only them. This is the only real achievement that is necessary. Accordingly, David Cameron does not really have to do anything to be progressive. He just has to gain a general acceptance that he is a progressive politician. And this is precisely why he has made the statements and taken the actions he has, and why Labour has tried so hard to label him by his privileged background and education and describe him as the 'same old Tory'. The idea of progress therefore should be seen as a badge, which shows that one is optimistic about the future and wishes to create change. The badge is worn to create a particular positive feeling and so give people a reason to vote.

But because it is a label rather than anything more substantive, the stakes are somewhat lower. Progress becomes an end in itself and so it never becomes a matter of success or failure. However, this means that the progressive never learns from their mistakes. They need never face up to the failure of their ideas. Their optimism never wanes and they feel that things will get better next time. Experience never tells with the progressive, because the abstract principles always supervene, always override the doubts. Optimism always seems to be better than pessimism, more promising as it were. Pessimism can always be dismissed as cynicism, and it always seems better to be positive instead of negative, to be looking forwards rather than backwards. So the leap of faith is taken again and the progressive goes through the same optimistic hope for the future, and when it falls flat they have the same surprised reaction as if things had never gone wrong before. But fortunately there is always a new project to move on to and so they summon up their enthusiasm and sense of purpose and off they go again, ignoring the 'cynical' and 'negative' criticism. The art of the progressive involves never standing still, never being caught and made to explain what they have or have not done. As a result there is a positive incentive to ensure that progress is continuous and that there is no time to assess what happened in the past.

Change is perhaps accepted most readily when its consequences need not be feared. When people are affluent and comfortable, when they are well-shod, fed and housed, then there is less need to fear change. However, where there is only subsistence, where existence is precarious, any change from the status quo is justifiably to be feared. The consequences of change are far greater; they can be literally life threatening rather than merely inconvenient, and they certainly will not be seen as exhilarating.

Those who are affluent will have something of a cushion which gives them the ability to deal with change. They have some margin because they have the resources to help combat any adverse consequences. The affluent can mitigate the effects of change, and bad decisions or unforeseen happenings are not so consequential. There is a security that leads to a sanguine attitude to change. Risk is manageable and even perhaps to be welcomed as providing something different, a welcome entertainment even. But for those already on the edge, where basic subsistence is the priority, change is a disaster; it can throw everything else out. This point is well made by Joyce Appleby (2010) at the very start of her history of capitalism. She argues that for those who constantly feared famine, change was something to be resisted and to worry over. The perception was that any change would be for the worse, a potential disaster. Appleby points out that it was this very resistance to change that held back the development of capitalism. What is feared here is not change of something specific, but the very notion of change itself: there is a belief that change is bad by definition. Again it is the very non-specificity of change that causes concern.

Perhaps there is a parallel with politics in the USA and the tea party movement we discussed in the introduction. President Obama, as we have seen, campaigned as the change candidate and won handsomely in November 2008. He captured the imagination of many even as the recession deepened in the USA and throughout the world. Yet after a year of his attempts to deal with this recession Obama's stock had fallen considerably. The changes he has sought to introduce, such as health care reform, an economic stimulus package and a cap-and-trade policy to limit climate change, have proved to be unpopular with large sections of the American people, including many who voted for him in 2008. What many people focused on was the higher levels of debt and increase in unfunded government spending as a result of the health care proposals and the stimulus package. The protesters felt that they were taxed enough already (hence the 'tea' in tea party). This led to some resurgence of support for Republicans, but more worrying for Washington is that these protests seemed to be part of a relatively autonomous movement.

As the recession worsened in the USA, the attitudes of many Americans to the idea of change, and consequently towards the change candidate, hardened and a more negative perception of Obama developed. The president who had appeared to offer so much promise for change had lost his golden appeal in only a year. Of course, this may not be fatal, in that a similar slump occurred in President Clinton's first-term fortunes only for him to be re-elected comfortably. However, it does suggest that change is often better served up in a benign environment rather than during a recession.

Of course, several of the changes that worry the tea party protesters are quite clearly seen by them as changes for the worse: people fear they are being made worse off and that their country is being altered. This might suggest a particular attitude towards change: in a recession we see change as negative as it will always be for the worse. But the changes proposed by Obama are not intended to make people worse off. Part of the economic stimulus package was a tax cut for the majority of taxpayers and the proposals to extend health care provision can be argued to be a benefit for society as a whole. However, these changes were not perceived by these protesters in this manner. Instead they concentrated on the government's inability and unpreparedness to repay the public debt and apparent shift away from a low tax economy (O'Hara, 2010).

The attitude towards Obama might have a number of causes. First, it might be that his policies have neither been well thought out or sensible. Second, the conditions in which these changes are being made might be creating the negativity. Recessions and financial turmoil might not be the best time to convince taxpayers of the need for billions of dollars of extra spending. But third, we might suggest that change is often more welcome in the abstract, when we are listening to a range of candidates and considering who should receive our vote. We might feel that we want the changes being proposed, especially when there is no price tag attached or accurate sense of the upheaval that might result. So we might want change until it actually occurs and we are faced with the bills and the uncertainty of new arrangements and the ending of long established and trusted ways of operating. When Obama spoke of change it was hypothetical: he was 'not-Bush', and could present himself as being fundamentally different. He said he would change many things and did not need to provide many details of what he would do, how he would change things and what it would mean. He could focus on the positive consequences and downplay the negative. But in office this is no longer possible: now change has to be costed and the President is the one held responsible. He could promise to close the Guantanamo Bay prison camp and take the applause on the campaign trail. But when in office he then had to decide what to do with terrorists still considered a threat to the USA, but who might have been captured using illegal methods and with information inadmissible in court, and who cannot be returned to their own countries. Any decision Obama takes in office has specific and tangible effects on real people, which involves the redistribution of resources, the setting of priorities and the taking of sides. There are winners and losers, perceptions are created, friends and enemies made and calculations need to be made about the prospects for re-election. Change is suddenly very consequential.

What might mitigate this problem for us is if we knew we would remain in control and be instrumental in forming any new order; that we could, so to speak, be on the 'right' side of change. This might lead us to seek or accede to change with more equanimity. In this situation the change would be ours, we would control it and be in the best position to benefit from it. But, of course, few of us are, or could be, in such a position where we can state what changes are to be made and when we should stop. Most of us are passengers and not drivers.

But even if we were in the driving seat this presupposes that we can predict what will occur and that change will remain predictable. We can be in control of our vehicle, but not of those in front or behind us, let alone the one coming straight towards us. In a complex society we can never exert such a level of control where we can accurately predict outcomes. We might be in the best position to profit, but this is only if things work out as we expect them to. If we actually do not control all eventualities, if we cannot limit the influences and the incidents along the way, then we may not be left with outcomes which we intended.

Yet despite the problems with the progressive attitude it is highly unlikely that any politician would actively seek to be seen to be against progress. It is not seen as a vote winner or a means of success. The issue here is that politicians believe they can never go backwards, but only forwards. Politicians will claim that they seek organised and planned change – politicians, as we know (because this is what they tell us), only ever do things for a considered reason – and do not just react. However, in practical terms, much of politics is precisely about reacting to situations, be it a natural disaster, an economic crisis, foreign aggression, a scandal or a drop in popularity. Politics is very much about reacting to events. Neither President Bush nor Prime Minister Blair expected or wanted to be war leaders when they took office. Indeed both put much greater emphasis on a domestic reform agenda. In both the USA and the UK, however, much of this reform was not achieved, partly because of opposition, but also because the priorities shifted after September 11, 2001. The same can be said of Mrs Thatcher's governments, for whom privatisation developed out of necessity, and whose image was transformed by the Falklands war, an event that could not have been predicted when Mrs Thatcher had been elected three years earlier. Of course, these politicians all had different starting points, and were predisposed towards particular solutions, but much of what they were actually able to do was prescribed by circumstance.

We should not expect any government, whatever its political stripe, to be any different from its predecessors in this respect. Any government will be constrained by circumstance, some of which are already known (public finances in the decade after 2010 will be extremely tight, and government spending will need to be cut), but many of the events that will motivate action in the future years of a government are as yet unknown, and this is quite simply because these events are yet to happen. Just as Bush could not have foreseen the events of September 11 and the impact that this would have on his presidency, his successors can have no idea what will impact on them.

So, politics, to a great extent, is about reacting to events. But this is not something most politicians would wish to acknowledge and nor would they see it as a virtue. However, it is inevitable. Politicians might not openly accept this, and some are better than others at hiding it (compare Thatcher and Blair with the floundering of Major and

Brown), but all spend much of their time reacting to events rather than fulfilling a positive programme.

What would seem to make a difference between politicians is where they start from: what are their core principles, what motivated their interest in politics and desire to seek election, and so what options are never considered or only seen as a last resort? These core principles will help determine their attitudes towards, say, state ownership or privatisation, and so how will they react to a crisis needing their intervention.

However, this is very much complicated by how a politician thinks they will be perceived by the electorate and so what they feel is expected of them in particular circumstances. The result of this might be that the politician acts in a way that is the opposite of their assumed natural inclination. So, for example, in 2008 Prime Minister Gordon Brown, by nature an egalitarian and part of the authentic socialist Labour tradition in a way that Tony Blair never was, was apparently so frightened of the concept of nationalisation that he persuaded Lloyds TSB bank to take over its struggling competitor, HBOS, even though it has proved to be near suicidal for Lloyds and has cost government billions of pounds in guarantees and bailouts (King, 2010b). Similarly, President Obama seemed determined not to nationalise banks or carmakers, not because he was particularly ideologically against nationalisation – he was presumed to be in favour of it – but because it would seem to prove what his critics had always claimed, namely that Obama was a closet socialist. Both Brown and Obama did not want to give credence to what their opponents were saying of them, and so did what was apparently against their principles. On the opposite side of the spectrum it would have been hard to predict that President Bush, considered one of the most right-wing presidents in US political history, would himself have nationalised financial institutions in 2008. But he must have felt that there was no alternative to do what he would have hoped was only a temporary measure. Of course, it might have helped him that these events occurred in the last six months of his second term. He would not, then, be around to deal with the fall-out and nor did he need to stand to account before the electorate. Whether he would have acted the same in the first year of his term is open to speculation, but it was clear that Bush looked at the situation in front of him, took advice and reacted (Paulson, 2010). These examples show how perceptions matter in terms of how politicians react. Their principles could apparently take second place to the expediency of reacting to a crisis.

Importantly we do not assume that these actions were irresponsible or reprehensible. We might question their specific judgements, albeit with the benefit of hindsight, but we do not complain that they reacted. Indeed we would have found it odd if they would have put their principles before all else and refused to recognise that crises call for special attention.

This might help explain the lure of progress. In democratic politics, perceptions matter, as well as how those perceptions are managed. We saw this from the Conservatives both before and after the 2010 election. As we shall consider in Chapter Five, their manifesto exhibited optimism and downplayed the problems to be faced in terms of deficit reduction, job losses and tax increases. Once the election was out of the way and the coalition formed, we saw a more realistic and downbeat focus with a much greater emphasis on debt reduction. Before the election the Conservatives wished to stress their idea of the Big Society, but afterwards they told the electorate that all the government's commitments would be dependent on the state of the public finances. But this sense of managing perceptions is not restricted to Cameron in 2010. The Conservatives when led by Mrs Thatcher attempted to suggest Britain was in the midst of a crisis and facing a final opportunity to pull away from the brink of disaster. The Conservatives here wished to persuade the electorate that they must be given the opportunity to govern and that this was an absolute imperative.

So we should admit that politics turns on the management of perceptions, and this is why the idea of progress – the clarion call of a better future – will always have its appeal. And this, we have to admit, will be the case with the Conservatives as with any other party. Of course, understanding the lure of progress does not mean that we should accept it is as an imperative. We might still remain sceptical of the pull of the future and wish to look backwards instead. Indeed, for many this might actually have a positive appeal.

THREE

Reacting to change

Introduction

If we see the modern world as complex and if we believe that understanding it is difficult and even perplexing, then why should we seek to change it? If we do not know what would happen if we pulled this lever or pressed that button why would we do it? If we cannot understand certain processes why should we seek to encourage them? Where would the benefit be for us? Why should a Conservative politician like David Cameron see it as a good thing, as beneficial, to state categorically that he is in favour of progress when it is not possible to know what will occur as a result?

It might be, as we have suggested, because it shows that the Conservative party has changed. They are no longer the 'nasty party', but are now part of the 'progressive consensus'. Just like the Labour party, they wish to create a better society for us all to live in. By aping their opposition they can then show that they have changed fundamentally. This might not please their core vote, the backwoodsmen and blue rinses in the shires, but where are they going to go? It is assumed that the core vote will turn out and support the party, if only to get rid of a Labour government, and because they would prefer their party to anything else, even if it is making some new and disturbing sounds. Therefore, the party leadership feels it can ignore this group, and perhaps even insult it from time to time, and focus instead on pacifying and persuading floating voters and those who have not supported the party for some time. In this regard we should note that a so-called 'core vote strategy' – of appealing to one's natural supporters – is often seen as a sign of desperation, of ensuring that their natural voters all come out and support the party and so prevent a landslide (Bale, 2010). As was shown by the Conservative party's poor performance in the 2001 and 2005 elections, it is a tactic unlikely to succeed, compared to a broad church approach that seeks to gain and maintain a wide coalition of support.

But even if the Conservatives had not developed a rhetoric of progress prior to the election, they had a clear incentive to do so afterwards. The Liberal Democrats are an avowed progressive party, who see themselves as left of centre. In order to successfully woo them and maintain a relationship the Conservatives therefore have clear reasons for developing notions of fairness, social justice and progress.

This, of course, is to see progress as being about image. It is to present a particular view of how we see society progressing to something better and so giving hope for the future. We have to take this accusation seriously, because modern politics is increasingly about presentation and creating a particular image or feeling. Politicians may disparage this and call for a concentration on policy and 'the issues that matter to people', but this is usually to criticise their opponents' presentation while spending more on their own. It is believed that political parties have to cultivate an image that is appealing to a plurality of voters and so they need to remain in touch with popular culture, follow the mainstream media and listen to the focus groups.

But what is this process of following trends if it not a form of reaction? Indeed, as we have seen, David Cameron justified modernising the Conservative party on the basis that it has to appeal to Britain as it is, and not how it used to be or how the party might wish it to be (Bale, 2010). This is therefore merely a form of reaction, of responding to circumstance, even if the outcome is to claim a progressive agenda.

But if progress can be written off as merely a matter of presentation how should we take the idea of reaction? Should we also see this as a matter of image only, of putting forward a particular persona that is calculated to achieve a given effect? Of course, most reactionaries would find the very idea of being image conscious as offensive. But if, as we have seen, reactionaries do not prevent all change, and if reactionaries such as Burke are prepared to admit that change might even be necessary, then what is the point of holding out against it? Is what self-confessed reactionaries are doing merely a 'show' of reaction, a demonstration of one's disapproval of change and a desire to keep as much as possible as it is, but which, in reality, is nothing more than image creation?

There may be examples of this, although the sheer unfashionableness of reactionary ideas might lead one to question anyone's reasoning for holding such a position. One way around this problem, which would work equally well for the progressive Conservative and the reactionary, is to resist seeing these categories as being of the 'all or nothing' variety. One need not be a progressive in all things and all of the time, and nor must a reactionary oppose each and every change that is ever proposed. Both positions are much more nuanced than this, partly to create a particular effect or perception, but mainly in that the attitude is targeted at specific proposals and ideals rather than change in general.

So the reactionary might see their role not as trying to stop all and every change, but to act as something as a brake on change. We often use a brake not to stop, but to slow ourselves down. This ensures that we remain safe and comfortable and that we have not taken any unnecessary risks. We are not disconcerted by jerky changes and so do not fear a crash. Our journey is smooth and uneventful and this is important to us because it means we can focus on where we are going. The journey has allowed us to arrive at our destination where our purposes can be fulfilled. Perhaps we see change in these terms, not as a permanent condition but as a transition. We perceive a change as a temporary state, as a movement from one place to another. However, being in transit is not where we want to be. We have left somewhere and wish to be somewhere else. The change is perhaps necessary – it might be unavoidable – but it is not our main purpose. We are moving for a reason, which may make things better (although we might be changing because we have no choice). But what is important is to get from A to B, to make the transition, and to do so as conveniently and comfortably as possible. So change is not something to relish but to be got over and to be put behind us so we can return to our routines and habits again.

Of course, a politician would find little support were they to claim to be in favour of transition, or a dislocation, or to suggest we should remain in that nether state between two points. But this is what change or progress actually amounts to. It is a transition, rather than a stable point. It is uncertainty itself, a move from one fixed point to another, where what we want may well be these fixed points. This means that the actual language of progress is very important and politicians are careful in how they portray change. It must be planned and foreseen and, most important, it must always be a change for the better. This might sound obvious, but progressives must be able to suggest that a change will be an improvement and not the creator of distress or uncertainty. As we have suggested, what allows them to do this is the very hypothetical nature of the future: the future can always be painted as golden whereas we can see the tarnished present for what it actually is. Hence we return to the nature of presentation and the manner in which progressives are able to present change as being a promise and not a liability.

As we have seen, there is a tendency to see change as always positive and to view opposition to it as cynical or negative, or even divisive. It is always better to seem to be positive and open to new things, rather than resisting them and trying to keep things as they are. But might there not be a real virtue in scepticism and resistance, of trying to maintain stability and preserve what works, especially if what we are doing is not preventing all and every change but ensuring that changes only occur to preserve what is important? We might wish to keep things as they are because they have stood the test of time. There are institutions, agencies and ways of acting that have been around for many years, perhaps centuries, and we know that they work. They have served us well and we know what their utility is. We may accept that they are not perfect, and that if we were ever able to start again (which we know we will never be able to do), or create the ideal world (assuming we could ever agree what that might involve), we might make them differently (assuming we knew how to). But we know that we cannot start from scratch. We cannot, practically speaking, go back to year zero, at least not without huge upheaval and distress. We can only start from where we are, and with what we have got and so we need to determine what works for us and what we might therefore be sacrificing should we lose it.

This is the very opposite of the progressive's use of the future. Unlike the assumption that what we do not know about must be better than what we do, the reactionary assumes that if the present is not perfect then nor will be the future. The present, however, has the great virtue that we know what we have, we know what our life is like, what we enjoy and what to avoid. We have our roots, our sense of self, our habits, traditions and accepted ways of doing things. And why, knowing what we do, should we change these patterns? How could it benefit us to throw up the structures and patterns of our life for the unknown and as yet unknowable? Why should we take the risk? It is clearly possible to answer all these questions with reasons in favour of progress and change. But these would not necessarily convince the reactionary. This is because they do not believe that the promise of the future can be better that the actuality of the present. They will believe that they have the concrete evidence to support this view, but that is not the most important consideration for them. Their position is based on an attitude, a particular disposition, and this cannot be readily gainsaid.

In this chapter we shall look at reaction and traditionalism as a political idea. I therefore wish to take the idea of conservation very seriously and assess whether reaction has any appeal at all. I also want to open up the question of whether what Cameron is doing is really the polar opposite of reaction. I wish to assess how far the decision to form a coalition was based on a shared progressive agenda and how much was actually a reaction to circumstance. This is important because, as we shall see in the following chapters, much of the opposition to the coalition did not come from the Liberal Democrats or the left of the Conservative party, but from the right; from commentators and politicians who felt that Cameron had let down his natural supporters and deserted the 'true' path of conservatism.

A nice equipoise

As we have seen, the problem with the search for progress is that it tends to ignore or, at best, to disdain what we have now. The present is not good enough; it is imperfect and could be improved upon. It is always possible to point to what is wrong with the current arrangements, be it an unrepresentative voting system, an outdated House of Lords based on the hereditary principle, or the unequal distribution of wealth. The fact that no system is ever perfect gives the progressive a continual excuse to call for change. They can always suggest that the future, which they purport to see all planned out before them, will be better for us. In consequence, the effort of the progressive goes in proselytising for this future better way. But this might well mean that they are forced to spend so much of our time planning and creating the perfect future that they actually forget to live now. They are so busy planning to be elsewhere that they miss out on what is good about their lives here and now. And because, as history shows, they might fail to create anything better, all their efforts might actually be in vain. So they fail to live now, choosing instead to campaign for what does not currently and might never exist, and to forego happiness now for the hypothetical prospect of happiness to come. They are so busy plotting and planning that they forget to live, love and care now.

This might be acceptable if it merely involved the few progressive activists pushing for change on their own account. But they do not wish merely to live the better life themselves: they want it for all of us in the sincere belief that it is for our own good. Therefore, their efforts are as much about reforming the rest of us as looking after themselves. Thus where progressives are successful they change the lives of everyone.

Yet for many simply living now is enough and it is all we seek. We accept that things could be better, and this might, all things being equal, be preferred, but we know that it is not likely we will attain this new world and do not wish to put at risk all we have for it. We are not prepared to risk everything we have for the possibility of a better future. We might prefer just to be left alone.

Clearly there would be a point where we would take the risk, if our present life became so bad, or the prospective pay-off of change was great enough. Our current existence might be so poor that we are prepared to go along with plans for reform. But even here we might retain some reservations. We might be concerned to know how certain the pay-off might actually be, and what level of control we might have over any changes. We might want to be assured that there is an escape route if things started to go wrong: can we say 'no' and go home if we change our minds?

Perhaps what worries us is that we know that these controls are not available. We realise that change is often a one-way process, which does not allow for an opt-out or a change of mind. We fear that when the promised land is arrived at, and it proves to be barren and less than we had hoped for, we have no recourse and no means of retracing our tracks. Change, all too often, is one-way and this adds to the uncertainty. As we saw when we discussed Joyce Appleby's view of change in pre-capitalist societies (Appleby, 2010), if we are at the bottom now, and as far as we can remember that is where people 'like us' have always remained, why should we expect the future to be different? Unlike those who are comfortable and have some leeway, we might have everything to lose by following idealists towards their vision of progress.

Utopias cannot be tested. They can be made to sound absolutely wonderful and full of promise. But change is always more difficult than expected. The reason for this is that we can only start from where we currently are. We do not have level ground and perfect building blocks. We are not empty-headed innocents able to be programmed to accept new ways of thinking suitable for the new world being made for us. Instead we are complex individuals with existing aspirations, expectations and prejudices who are used to operating within a complex set of institutions which we have only an incomplete understanding of. Creating change is therefore very difficult, as is described by Edmund Burke in his 'Thoughts on the Present Discontents':

> Our Constitution stands on a nice equipoise, with steep precipices and deep waters upon all sides of it. In removing it from a dangerous leaning towards one side, there may be a risque of oversetting it on the other. Every project of a material change in a Government so complicated as ours, combined at the same time with external circumstances still more complicated, is a matter full of difficulties; in a which a considerate man will not be too ready to decide; a prudent man too ready to undertake; or an honest man too ready to promise. They do not respect the publick nor themselves, who engage for more than they are sure that they ought to attempt, or that they are able to perform. (Burke, 1999a, p 142)

This is a further, and extremely elegant, restatement of the 'tightrope' view of politics we have encountered already. Burke reminds us that caution is needed because governing is such a difficult process, both because of internal and external factors which play on the body politic. In consequence we should not seek to over-stretch, to go too far in our plans for fear of upsetting what is a finely balanced situation. The role of the politician is to recognise and respect these limits. The risks of over-stretching are too great; we may tumble down the steep precipices and into the deep waters. Burke notes that it is not just the politician who might fall, but that they risk taking everything and everyone with them.

A conservative therefore ought to be cautious in their attitude to change. This does not mean that conservatism need be reactionary per se. It can be forward looking, and as we know, Burke said that a state needs the means of change in order to preserve itself. But this merely shows what, and only what, change should be reserved for. We should not seek the grandiose plan, but to change only when it is necessary to maintain ourselves in the way we are accustomed. This would suggest that we cannot be a progressive and remain coherently conservative. We cannot see change as an end in itself and be consistently conservative. Change is a means to preserve and only that.

So if a conservative need not be a reactionary, but cannot be a progressive, where does this leave us? One suggestion might be to argue that the ideal for a conservative would be to remain neutral between reaction and progress. The response of a conservative ought to be contingent to circumstance and therefore dependent on the particular situation. When the situation changes so should the conservative. But, of course, this might imply it is entirely acceptable to adopt the jargon of one's opponents, and hence try to call oneself a progressive and, in doing so, prove we are reactionary! We cannot, it seems, get beyond presentation in practical politics.

Reaction

But are we doing full justice to the concept of reaction? Why, in particular, has it been so closely connected with conservatism? It might, therefore, pay to consider reaction in more detail. The first thing we should say is that reaction is not just opposition. Reaction is a response to something concrete. It is against something and not just against all things. It is targeted and specific, the result of some event, or the fear of something. Hence Joseph de Maistre (1974, 1993) was not reacting against all and everything, but rather a particular set of changes brought about by the ideas of the philosophes, the Enlightenment, the French Revolution and the resulting regicide. The same applies to Edmund Burke (1999b, 1999c), who responded to the events in France, the consequent war in Europe and what he saw as the appeasing attitudes of the British government to the threat of French expansionism.

The use of cognates such as 'obscurantist' and 'blimpish' implies a sense of being outside of the mainstream and occupying some dark corner away from the normal flow of life. We are left with an image of the reactionary standing out against everything, their back against the wall seeking to hold off all and every change. But, of course, this is not what a reaction is at all. In science the word 'reaction' actually means a change, and often a violent one. For a chemist a reaction is a response caused by a particular stimulus. Two compounds are introduced to each other and there is a reaction. This coming together of two different elements forces a response that leaves neither element in its previous state. The two elements react to form something new and different. An explosion, with all its consequences, is a reaction. So, in this sense, reaction is not about going backwards. Indeed strictly speaking, it is *a progression* beyond what had previously existed.

In the social and political sense we should therefore see a reaction as a causal response. It comes about in answer to some other phenomena. The aim of this reaction might be to stop something, to prevent an unwanted change, but this result might be a new and different social order which is an amalgam of the initial state and the attempt at progress.

However, the analogy with chemistry can only go so far. We cannot say that a chemical reaction is animated by any purpose. It happens because of the nature of the elements involved and their relative compatibility or incompatibility. But humans act for a reason and to achieve something. We do not respond automatically, although some of us might be more predisposed towards resisting change than others. However, whatever our predisposition, we have been provoked. The reason for the reaction is unlikely to be to create a new synthesis, but to stop anything changing at all.

But the very act of resistance can create change, as appears to be the case in the USA with the tea party movement's reaction to President Obama's policies. The intervention of the tea party movement has shifted political debate, led to the rejection of certain Republican candidates and changed the nature of political discourse in the US. Therefore a reaction might be both an attempt to pre-empt the consequences of change and itself the cause of further change.

This complicates our sense of what reaction might be and suggests that there is more to it than merely saying no. The result of reaction might be, for want of a better word, a progression. This returns us to the idea of neutrality as a possible way out of this dilemma. Instead of being against something, perhaps it would be better to take a neutral stance. We should place our emphasis on stability, steadiness and slowness. Instead of seeking to do anything we should instead rely on neglect and drift. These are seen as negatives, easily portrayed as apathy and a lack of interest. But we should not necessarily see these terms always as negatives. Or perhaps, neglect and drift are useful precisely because they are negative. They slow down change, act as resistance, albeit of an essentially passive kind. We should recall again here Ronald Reagan's aphorism: when there is a call for government action to some issue or problems he suggested that we should shout in response, 'Don't just do something, stand there'. It is assumed that doing something is preferable than doing nothing, and it is very difficult for a politician to respond to a crisis by sitting on their hands. Yet this idea of doing 'something, anything' is precisely the sort of knee-jerk reaction that progressives use to caricature their opponents: 'just do something' is a panic reaction to a crisis.

We should see no necessary virtue in action per se. Rather what matters is why a particular action occurs. Is the action strictly necessary; does it have to happen, and if so, how can it be so managed as to ensure that its effects mesh in with our expectations? How can we ensure that this change only strengthens us and does not detract from what is important to us, and so does not weaken us? If we were to start from a questioning of the purpose of each and every change we would then actually be acting rationally and cautiously and in full awareness of the fragile equipoise of our position. This inevitably will put a brake on change. It might even be said to be a presumption against change, and so we might conclude that we are not really being neutral at all.

However, we need to remember that we are not here calling for exclusivity. We are not suggesting that this is what all people will or even must believe. Rather what this presumption against change will do is to balance those who presume that a change is always better than the status quo. It presents this view with a challenge and the result might be some compromise. In other words, and to return to our chemical analogy, we are seeking to create a controlled reaction. What we are seeking to do is to place a brake on change to ensure that we preserve what is important and do not lose it in a rush for what is new and untried.

I would suggest that this links with the actuality of practical politics. It is far easier to deal in absolutes, of two sides divided by clear blue or red water that stand by readily identifiable principles. Yet politics is actually rather messy and is based on a succession of compromises caused by circumstance. The Conservatives could not achieve a majority in Parliament in May 2010 and the Liberal Democrats were unable to capitalise on their successful campaign and achieve the breakthrough they had sought and thought they might achieve. Yet both parties are now in government, as they desired. They may not be doing all they wished to do, and are perhaps doing some things they would rather not. The Conservatives have dropped their support of marriage through the tax system, while the Liberal Democrats are part of a government committed to serious cuts in public expenditure, keeping Britain's nuclear deterrent and removing schools from local authority control. Both sides in the coalition are seeking to protect their interests while responding to a set of circumstances they did not wish for but could not prevent. The two parties are, properly speaking, reacting to circumstance.

As we have suggested, reactionaries such as Burke did not necessarily oppose all change. Instead they saw reaction as a form of pragmatism aimed at preserving the vital elements of a society. Part of this was because they saw these elements as being under threat, but this does not mean that they exercised restraint in their positions. Some reactionaries might oppose all change, but this is actually a very rare position to take.

Instead, as we have consistently stated, reactionary thinkers acknowledge that change is inevitable, but wish to ensure that its consequences are not too drastic and that no healthy flesh is removed along with the cancerous tissue. Burke in his writings on Ireland, India and on slavery saw the need for reform and change, but only over time and in a controlled manner (Burke, 1999d). He put forward proposals leading towards the abolition of slavery, but he sought to do this in a way that did not completely overturn the social and economic arrangements of the time. This might be seen as delay for those who could not abide the iniquity of slavery, but Burke was concerned with what might come after slavery and how would both former slaves and those dependent on the trade and its industries cope with its abolition. Likewise, he argued that Catholics should be able to participate in Irish politics and elections, but not by tearing down those parts of the Constitution which protected property rights and the established relations between Church, the State and its citizens. As Burke argued in defending the British Constitution as it stood in 1782, despite its apparent lack of representativeness: 'It is for fear of losing the inestimable treasure we have, that I do not venture to game it out of my hands for the vain hope of improving it' (1999d, p 30). He does not rule out change, but merely asks us to focus on what we might lose in rushing to deal with an apparent inequity. We should see them as examples of an attempt to devise a humane and sustainable situation that allowed change where it was needed but which preserved what deserved to be kept. This will certainly not satisfy the progressive, and nor will it necessary sound pleasing to one with twenty first century sensibilities, but we should recognise that Burke was concerned with the attitudes and problems of his time. Burke wanted to ensure that we do not lose the good things in our rush to end the bad.

In more contemporary circumstances we should recognise that politicians tend to act incrementally, ensuring that they maintain popular support and take people along with them. Hence the proposals of the coalition to reform welfare will be introduced over a ten-year period to ensure that the disruptions are not too great and that there are no (or not too many) losers (Department for Work and Pensions, 2010). This may mean that reform will be messy and open to compromise as circumstances change over time. It also might disconcert those who suggest that the government is not moving fast enough to deal with welfare dependency. However, we might suggest that we are more certain of arriving safely at our destination by taking many small and manageable steps rather than attempting one risky and dramatic leap.

So it is reasonable to argue that all politics is, to a greater or lesser extent, about reaction. But is there really no difference between being reactive, in the sense of having to respond to events, and being a reactionary? A reactionary, because they are set firmly on a particular path, might actually not react at all, but try to stay consistent, bent on achieving the general acceptance of their particular set of principles over and above every other condition. But this might also be the case with those overly besotted with progress, who put their plans over everything else. Examples might be Mao and Stalin, who respectively put their 'great leap forward' and five-year plans above the realities of daily life and the actual conditions of their citizens. Even mass starvation did not cause them to alter their course. This rigid following of principle at the expense of all else is reminiscent of the caricature of the reactionary.

But we might just be confusing here a particular attitude with the consistency of purpose with which it is applied. There are some reactionaries who will hold out against all forms of modernity, just as there are progressives who are immune to caution and calculation. But we should not necessarily take these as demonstrative of their kind. As we have stated sufficiently often already, reactionaries are not opposed to all and every change, and likewise not many (if any) progressives take a fundamentalist 'year zero' approach to change. One can prefer reform to revolution, just as others might prefer negotiation to a fight to the death.

But this should not be taken to mean that reaction is mere expedience and has no principles behind it. We should not see a reactionary as being irrational, even if they are opposed to the particular rationalism of the French Enlightenment. Thinkers like Joseph de Maistre and Edmund Burke used reason to substantiate their opinions. They did not simply assert their opinions or flail about in anger, but instead sought to put forward a reasoned argument against particular changes or to call for a return to a previous situation. They presented arguments which were aimed at countering progressive opinion, and, because these were reasoned views, they themselves demanded clear reasoning if they were to be countered. De Maistre, it is true, has been accused of fanaticism and madness (Lebrun, 1988; Berlin, 1990). However he was a highly cultured and learned intellectual who wrote in particularly elegant prose style. He was certainly determined in his principles and so he might well be called, as Richard Lebrun (1988) does, an intellectual militant, but this takes nothing away from the quality of his thought. Burke, we might suggest, has been even more influential and frequently read, perhaps because he is more measured in his prose and his arguments. Burke, who might not have thought of himself as a reactionary (at least not until the very end of his life), is an entirely civilised thinker, and importantly, one who cultivated a coherent set of ideas and a political movement which is now referred to as conservatism (in the British and American sense). He was perhaps the first to achieve a consistent description of what we might see as modern conservatism and he did so in a manner that it both elegantly presented and intellectually consistent with the principles and disposition he seeks to detail. He offers no abstract theory, but provides a conservative approach to dealing with specific problems and issues and through this a means by which we can understand change and the need of a culture for its own traditions and history. Burke is able to explain how communities develop their own ways of operating and do so not by active design or on the basis individual action. Rather it is how actions meld together over time, given the freedom and space that continuity brings. As Burke tells us:

> [A] nation is not an idea only of local extent, and individual
> momentary aggregation, but it is an idea of continuity,
> which extend in time as well as in numbers, and in space.
> And this is a choice not of one day, or one set of people, not
> a tumultuary and giddy choice; it is a deliberate election of
> ages and of generations; it is a Constitution made by what
> is ten thousand times better that choice, it is made by the
> peculiar circumstances, occasions, tempers, dispositions,

and moral, civil, and social habitudes of the people, which disclose themselves only in a long space of time. It is a vestment, which accommodates itself to the body. Nor is prescription of government formed upon blind unmeaning prejudices – for man is a most unwise, and most wise, being. The individual is foolish. The multitude for the moment, is foolish, when they act without deliberation; but the species is wise, and when time is given to it, as a species it almost always acts right. (Burke, 1999d, p 21)

For Burke, it is accumulated wisdom that we should rely on rather than the current view or the opinion of the masses at any one point in time. We should see something as correct when it has stood the test of time and can therefore be relied upon. It is not just a passing vision or a momentary flash of apparent wisdom, but something which has been tested and found to retain its value.

Despite this it remains in the interests of the progressive to depict reactionaries as obscurantist, backward and unsophisticated, and to suggest that their reaction is a mere knee jerk or instinctive response to change that has no basis in reason or thought. It might well be the case that reactionaries come into their own when there is a strong sense of threat, when what they hold dear is perceived to be endangered. But, as a consequence, it is all too easy to associate reaction with negativity, with fear, dislike of the new, and hatred of the unknown and unfamiliar. Critics tend to use terms like 'horrified', 'disgust' and 'despised' with regard to how reactionaries apparently respond to ideas, as indeed Zeev Sternhell (2010) does when criticising anti-Enlightenment thinkers such as Burke, Johann Herder and de Maistre. Yet, in reality, these thinkers were much more positive and encouraging about their preferred systems. Where they reject change, they do so for sound reasons, because of their understanding of what we currently hold and what it would mean to lose them; about what certain institutions and traditions allow and why we should keep them. These thinkers revel in certain forms of social relations, which they see as uniquely beneficial, as being particularly tailored to certain ways of life. Accordingly, this way of life should not be caste off lightly.

Having said this, many of the arguments of reactionaries such as de Maistre can now be seen as wrong or outdated, be it throne and altar (de Maistre, 1850) or the inevitability of the executioner's role (de Maistre, 1993). De Maistre was sceptical of science and of what we now refer to as positivism and argued instead for a return to a more providential view of human social order (de Maistre, 1993, 1998).

This being so, why should we still read him? Partly it is because he is a great prose stylist, and partly because it is important to understand our intellectual antecedents. We read many figures from the past to understand our present, and this includes even those who might be said to have ended up on the losing side. But there is a more general and timeless reason: de Maistre demonstrates a particular caste of mind, a mentality that is properly reactionary. He is one of the best examples of a brilliant and cultured mind turned to maintaining a particular traditional sense of the world.

De Maistre's virtue is in his attempt to show the unvarnished reality of human nature, and so to provide a necessary counterweight to Enlightenment optimism and the idea that progress was inevitable. He shows us that progress can be destructive, and this is because of how human beings really are rather than what the French philosophes assumed them to be. Human beings, according to de Maistre, need order, discipline, constraint and punishment. He reminds us that wars happen and that some people relish them, and are proficient in prosecuting them, and that the rest of us rely on these people for our protection. We are glad when such people are there for us, even as we might be concerned about what they actually do in our name and we might not wish to delve too deeply into the full nature of their actions. In short, de Maistre shows that human beings are by no means perfect, nor are they perfectible, and this is not just some temporary aberration.

But also what the reactionary seeks to protect is by no means narrow and parochial. As Scruton (2007) shows, the culture that modern reactionaries try to defend, what might be called Western Civilisation, is based on broad principles, and is not, of course, merely the product of one culture:

> Civilisations grow out of and into each other, and often divide like amoebas so as to generate two contemporaneous offshoots; hence, it is very hard to set spatial or temporal boundaries on Western Civilisation. It grew from the fusion of Christianity with the law and government of Rome, became conscious of itself in the high Middle Ages, passed through a period of scepticism and Enlightenment, and was simultaneously spread around the globe by the trading and colonial interests of its more adventurous members. And throughout its most flourishing periods, Western Civilisation has produced a culture which rapidly absorbs and adapts the cultures of other places, other faiths and other times. Its basic fund of stories, its moral precepts, and

its religious imagery comes from the Hebrew Bible and the
Greek New Testament. Onto those Judeo-Christian roots,
however, has been grafted a tree of many branches, bearing
many kinds of fruit. The Thousand and One Nights, which
has a central place in Islamic culture, is equally part of the
cultural heritage of the West, while the pagan literature of
Greece and Rome has been taught for centuries as the fount
of our literary tradition (Scruton, 2007, p 3)

This civilisation, therefore is not a product of insularity, but its very
opposite. It is the result of an outward-looking search based on the
wonder of things around us. What reactionaries seek to protect therefore
is not just the result of a narrow inward-looking process but something
that is positively global and which has been built up over centuries. As
Scruton argues: 'it is important to understand, in the context of today's
"culture wars" and the widespread advocacy of "multiculturalism", that
Western culture has an unparalleled ability and willingness to assimilate
other cultural traditions' (2007, p 4).

What is being threatened therefore is not something based on just
one culture but which has a wide base and is the product of thousands
of years and possibly millions of minds. However, this does not stop
the threat to them, and much of Scruton's endeavours have been in
defending Western Civilisation from threats from the inside, from
what he terms a culture of repudiation, which seeks to undermine
the very basis of the western tradition. As a result his view tends to
be somewhat elegiac. He is concerned with the loss of much of our
culture and so his writing is tinged with a pessimistic sense that we
may already be too late to save our own heritage. This view is shared
by Joseph Ratzinger[1] and Marcello Pera (2006) in their discussion of
how Western Civilisation now appears increasingly to be 'without
roots'. They argue against the intellectual dominance of relativism,
postmodernity and the idea of progress. Ratzinger and Pera state that
in Europe and elsewhere we have a culture that is based on a clear
history with its roots in Athens and Jerusalem. We are part of a Greek
and Judeo-Christian tradition which we risk compromising by our
accommodation to other ideas such as liberal multiculturalism. They
portray Europe and America as tearing themselves apart from the inside
through a philosophy and politics of disenchantment and alienation.
Many in the West have become embarrassed and even ashamed of their
own culture and history and seek to replace it with something else.
But the result, as many conservatives would argue, is not actually to

replace one culture without another that is equally valid, but to leave a gaping hole, a void where nothing of significance is left.

Yet, there is much left to celebrate in Western culture and it is by no means all lost. Much of what Scruton, for instance, loves still exists to be uncovered and celebrated. In his works on aesthetics he is able to present a particular vision that maintains traditional virtues and the notion of the beautiful (Scruton, 1994, 2009). A particularly fine example is his essay entitled 'Eliot and conservatism' (Scruton, 2006). This is a profound and quite beautiful description of what is worth preserving in our own culture based on an acute reading of T.S. Eliot's poetry and his understanding of the meaning of culture. It is inspiring and affirming, and the very opposite of the hysterical and declamatory sense that reactionaries are often accused of deploying. He shows how Eliot is capable of mixing the rhythms of ordinary speech with the great traditions of European poetry. He reshaped the English language by bringing together the old and the new and in doing so he did not repudiate or seek to alienate as is common with modernist art, but to affirm the modern precisely by its connection, its very symbiosis, with the past. Scruton is here not arguing against anything, but seeking to explain what we actually still have and why we might still need it. Scruton, as in much of his writing, is here arguing for something and he is not merely an opponent of all that is new and untried. For him, there is enough in what we already have that remains available to us if only we would take the time to look.

It is therefore a mistake to equate reaction with backwardness or an uninformed view of the world. It may be that what motivates some reaction is fear, but it is often more considered than this. Or at least for the reactionary there is every reason for them to fear for the loss of certain things. But what they do not tend to do is disengage from the world. Reactionaries do not tend to retreat or refuse to participate in social and political life. Instead we should see reaction as a particular form of engagement, which may or may not be defensive. Often the reactionary is rather worldlier than the progressive, lacking, as they do, the latter's obsession with utopian abstraction. As the examples of Burke and de Maistre show, the reactionary is very much within the world, at the centre of things, stepping out with confidence to make their case. Reactionaries can most certainly be strident and even aggressive. Reaction is not to stand silent or simply to accept what they are given or what is currently occurring.

Likewise it is not the case that reaction leads to a fatalistic attitude. A simplistic view of reaction can lead to the conclusion that we should accept our fate and not seek to change anything. If we cannot predict the outcomes of change we should not accept any of it and so just take the consequences of being where we are. But fatalism might actually be inconsistent with reaction, in that to be fatalistic is to accept change rather than to reject it. Fatalism is not about accepting the status quo and fighting for it, but simply standing idle and doing nothing to protect what we hold dear. It is to be passive and to accept any change without any attempt to mitigate or prevent it. The fatalist accepts life on another's terms, and this is not acceptable to a reactionary who tends to know what they want and desires to keep it. Therefore reactionaries cannot be accepting, fatalistic or disengaged.

A more serious criticism of reaction is that it is bound to lose. As change always occurs, and it is only ever possible to delay or mitigate its effects, the reactionary is certain eventually to lose any battle they seek to join. It is certainly the case that we can view the history of the last two centuries as one progressive victory after another. This might suggest that reactionaries have not been particularly effective in holding back change. However, the situation is rather more complicated than this. It is precisely because reactionaries tend to lose that they still exist. If they were to win, assuming that we could decide what 'to win' might mean, and that all reactionaries could agree on this definition, this would put reactionaries out of business. The very reason that there are reactionaries is because of the persistence of the call for progress. There would be no need for reactionaries were it not for progress.

So, ironically, it is fortunate for the future of reaction that progress is always presumed to be needed. Progressives always see current arrangements as contingent and continually look to make further changes: utopia is always just in front of us, only slightly out of reach. Progressives always seem to exist and have a lot of work to do, and so they ensure that reaction is always needed.

What makes reaction particularly necessary is that progressives nearly always fail to deliver what they proclaim is inevitable. Progress is always prey to unintended or unforeseen consequences and unpredictability. Reactionaries are able to state with a high degree of certainty that things will go wrong. They may be unable to be specific and to say exactly what will go wrong, but it will be clear to them that things never go as planned and that much of the optimism of progressives is ill-founded. It is reasonable to state that progressives will misunderstand things, and that mistakes will be made by them. No one can understand every nuance and calculate every eventuality. This suggests that the reactionary's response is rooted in empirical evidence. It is based on the actual experience of the implementation of change. The fact that reactionaries tend to lose therefore only makes their view of the world more necessary and ensures that there is a place for reactionary thought. They can rely on the simple fact that progressives never learn.

We might state, therefore, that reactionary thought is the concrete statement of the actuality of practical politics. It is a statement of what actually occurs rather than relying on what ought to be. This brings us back to the issue of presentation in politics. We might argue, without undue cynicism, that the jargon of progress is underpinned by the realisation of the need and preparedness to react to changing circumstances in order to preserve our aims and intentions.

But this gives the thoughtful reactionary no place for complacency: the best they ever achieve is mitigation of the aims of the progressive. This might explain the elegiac nature we have already found in some conservative thought. English conservatives, like Scruton (2000, 2007, 2009), look back and see that much is now lost, and so the best they can do is to remember it before it is all forgotten. There is little in the way of anger or cynicism in this writing, just a sense perhaps of being let down, almost of the childishness and superficiality of progressives who toss away so much in their vain attempts to create a better tomorrow, whether it is in art, architecture, education or politics. The elegiac quality is because conservatives know that things could have been different, that we did know better but somehow allowed ourselves to be led along a potentially destructive route from which we cannot now return. We had the culture, the institutions and the enlightenment to prevent much of the change that we now regret. But we did not do enough to stop the destructive changes. This might lead to anger, but equally it may create a strong sense of regret and a strong desire to hold on to what appears to be fading.

This situation is perhaps an inevitable consequence of living in the present and with what we have now. We do not spend our time plotting and planning, and we are not seeking to control institutions and determine political action. We are busy elsewhere and so we leave the future to those who have a vision and a purpose and the drive to implement it. The conservative instead does not see the need to be continually questioning or justifying their place in the world. However, this attitude, as Richard Lebrun writes in his biography of Joseph de Maistre, presents a problem for the reactionary intellectual:

> Much of the strength of a traditional society lies in the fact that its structure and values are unquestioned – indeed unquestionable. It is only when the status quo has been attacked and disrupted that the need to defend it becomes imperative. The conservative theorist almost inevitably finds

himself in a defensive posture, involved in a debate on the relative merits of the old order versus the new, impelled to base his arguments on the assumptions of the innovators. And by engaging in the argument at all, he easily becomes suspect to members of the traditional elite who have always simply assumed the rightness of existing structures and values and their own privileged place in the traditional order. (Lebrun, 1988, p 124)

As de Maistre himself stated in *Against Rousseau* (1996, p 86): 'If a belief is not attacked, it would be useless to declare it'. Our beliefs only need expression when they are challenged, otherwise we could carry on without their articulation. Our beliefs become precious when they are attacked and we can no longer take them for granted. We are immersed in our world and do not recognise the importance of our way of life until it is under threat. Once our views are attacked we start to see them as distinct entities, as elements separate from us, yet very important, even crucial to us. They stop being merely part of us, or things just as they are, and instead become a distinct set of principles that need articulation in order to mount a defence. They have a meaning and a history. The principles become part of public discourse instead of being merely inchoate. We have to recognise what we have and what they mean, and the threat of their loss makes this all too clear to us.

The danger, of course, is that the conservative does not recognise what is being threatened, or is too complacent to react. As Lebrun (1988) pointed out, one may not even be thanked by our own side for articulating what it is we feel important and worth defending. The result is that we might exclude ourselves, and allow ourselves to become outsiders in our own culture because we do not notice what is being done on our behalf and, in any case, cannot understand why anyone would really want to do this. The reason for this situation is that, quite simply, the conservative accepts what they currently have. Unlike the progressive, the conservative does not see their current existence as contingent. For the conservative the present works as well as anything else, it does what they wish it to and they realise that we can thrive as well here as elsewhere. Our existence does not have to be a battle, or to be striving, to aspire, or to compete with others. Instead they argue that we should accept the world as it is and just live. In doing so, we will stop wasting the present for the hope of something in the future. We can work hard for the benefit of now, and not sacrifice now for what may never be.

So we can state that the key difference between progress and reaction is the attitude to the present, to how we live now. Do we find where we are now acceptable, can we live with it and do we feel that it accommodates us? Or are we dissatisfied; is what motivates us the feeling that our world could be so much better, such that we cannot tolerate leaving things as they are? We might say that the question turns on whether we see our lives here and now as enough, as something to be got on with and to make the best of, or whether we should use our time and our efforts to make for a better life. The progressive will see the effort worthwhile, whilst the reactionary would argue that what we now have is enough and, in any case, how can we know that the future will be better; how will we ever know that what is currently with us is not the best we can ever do?

Understanding conservatism

Academics and commentators have the luxury of sitting back and watching what politicians are doing. They can take their time and use hindsight to make their judgements. When they make predictions they are not necessarily held to them and they can change their minds with impunity. The consequences of a poor judgement for an academic or a journalist are really quite small and perhaps not much greater when their assessment is sound.

Academics, by their very nature, try to make sense of the world. They look for patterns, seek to codify, categorise, create and then use models and systems. Accordingly, in this discussion on conservatism and its manifestations as progressive and reactionary, we have tried to draw out some themes and concepts, and it is pertinent now to state these simply. First, conservatism can be seen as a disposition or an attitude rather than a set of definitive doctrines. It clearly can be conceptualised and ideas such as tradition, scepticism and organicism drawn out as typical of the various forms of conservatism that exist. But these concepts do not completely enclose what conservatism is: there remains something inchoate and beyond precise definition and this is precisely because conservatism is an approach, a reaction, to what is already out there. It is very much focused on the present and how we enjoy it. Of course, the jargon of Conservative politicians may detract from this understanding, but this, I would suggest, is of a part with the disposition.

This is because there is an underlying pragmatism within conservatism. Conservatives understand that politics is inherently reactive. This does not mean that many, if any, politicians see themselves as reactionary in the manner it is often portrayed. However, what they are involved in is the play of circumstance and the turn of events. Politics, as understood by the conservative, is the least abstract of activities.

This means, however, that there can be no completely successful attempt to define conservatism. There are most certainly general principles that might lead us in certain directions, but these are starting rather than end points. In particular, the actual actions of governments and political parties will be more complicated and nuanced than we can possibly capture. In any case, should we expect politicians to be circumscribed by theory and the attempts of academics to contain their actions within neat parameters? Conservatism, in particular, is about being actively engaged with the world as it currently is. Conservatives might not always like what they have to deal with, but they know they cannot change this without reason and consent.

Part of this pragmatism, as we have seen, is the importance of presentation in politics; of how a politician, Conservative or otherwise, is able to present him or herself towards the prevailing attitudes and sensibilities. It is this concern for presentation, which may be either overt or unconscious, that makes for the importance of the discourse of progress in modern politics.

The final element that we can draw from this discussion is that politics is about the creation of balance. It is the manufacturing of solutions through compromise, and particularly in the present, through coalition. Politics is the management of the 'nice equipoise' highlighted by Burke. It is a need to maintain some form of equilibrium in a precarious world with dangers all around. It is a concern for managing the impact of the unknown and unpredictable in order to maintain what is known and accepted.

This is the context in which we should address the 'new politics' of the Conservative–Liberal Democrat coalition formed in May 2010. What situation were these two parties faced with? What could they do but react in a manner that protected their interests and furthered their aims? This coalition was an attempt to react to the present, to balance that which appeared to be tilting, but within a discourse of politics which adhered to the idea of progress.

Note
[1] Cardinal Joseph Ratzinger, of course, became Pope Benedict XVI in 2005.

FOUR

Towards the new politics

Introduction

So on 11 May 2010 David Cameron could certainly claim success. He had just become the youngest Prime Minister for nearly 200 years and the Conservative party had been returned to power for the first time in 13 years. Yet Cameron's critics can also argue – and indeed have – that he had failed. He is not the head of a Conservative government but of a coalition with one of the parties he campaigned against during the election. The Conservative party failed to win enough seats for an overall majority despite a tired and unpopular government that was commonly seen to have failed. The Labour party suffered its second worst defeat since the Second World War, but still did sufficiently well to prevent an overall victory for the Conservatives.

In trying to adjudicate between these two views it rather depends on what one sees as important. If one is a critic of Cameron then one can suggest that he has failed to deliver on his promises. He argued that he should be allowed to modernise the party according to his own designs and in return he would provide victory at a general election. This, his critics suggest, he manifestly failed to do, and they claim that his modernisation of the party was therefore a mistake and that a more traditional agenda would have been more successful. This, of course, is a hypothetical and therefore unprovable argument, but, as we shall see, it was one that has been well aired in the press and on various right-of-centre blogs in the immediate post-election period.

On the other hand, David Cameron, the leader of the Conservative party, *is* the Prime Minister, and the majority of Cabinet posts, including the great offices of state, are held by Conservative politicians. And as Prime Minister, Cameron is just as powerful as he would have been if he had won an outright majority. Indeed he might actually be more powerful now with a majority in the House of Commons of over 80, and with nearly 60% of the electorate voting for the coalition parties.

This might mean that Cameron and his critics are both correct: it was a failure in one sense, but a success in another. What matters is how one views Conservatism and the importance of political power. As we shall see, one of the problems of the Conservatives since the early

1990s is that they have appeared to put the purity of their arguments and ideas above attaining power (Bale, 2010). This, as Ramsden (1998) has shown, is very untypical of the Conservative party. It is, however, a perfectly legitimate view to take: one wishes a certain position to prevail and too much compromise in order to attain power is pointless if it means jettisoning much of that position.

But whoever is correct in this (probably irresolvable) conflict, we can suggest that we are now in a period of what Cameron has been quick to call a 'new politics'. This was his avowed aim, and it is certainly true that things are now very different. The fall-out from the 2010 election has given us an untried government made up of politicians with very little ministerial experience from two apparently disparate parties, who are trying to govern in the middle of the biggest financial crisis since the Second World War. We are certainly, therefore, in an unusual and indeed peculiar situation in which many of the certainties of the previous few years have been cast away. The long period of economic growth, which began under the last Conservative government, has ended with a huge crash and the fall out from the complacency and hubris of that period is only now being recognised and addressed (King, 2010c). Much of the 'newness' facing the Cameron government is that of dealing with a different set of economic conditions from those they had expected. Immediately after his election as party leader in 2005, David Cameron sought to re-brand his party and to soften its image with a focus less on hard economic issues and more on matters such as climate change, civil liberties and well-being. His message was one of optimism, that the newly changed Conservatives could develop and extend the Blair legacy, using the same benign economic conditions, to form a more socially cohesive society (Bale, 2010; Snowdon, 2010). Cameron's emphasis was about putting what might be called 'lifestyle' issues above economic ones, on the assumption that the economy was rather nicely taking care of itself.

Since 2008 this optimism has no longer been tenable and the Conservatives have had to shift their focus back to managing the economy and the public finances. Accordingly, after the election, the new government talked of a new politics based on the national rather than narrow party interest, of putting the country first and of making difficult choices. The rhetoric was now of the country needing to pull together and so it was appropriate for two apparently opposed political parties, one from the right, the other from the left, to form a formal coalition to see the country through this period of difficulty.

Clearly such new politics was based on expedience: no party had an outright majority and the electoral mathematics pointed to only two realistic possibilities: a minority Conservative government, or a Conservative–Liberal Democrat coalition. We might suggest, therefore, that the call for a new politics was based on little more than narrow party interest. It was in the interests of both the Conservatives and Liberal Democrats, who had polled less well than they might have expected during the election campaign, to form this coalition, and to make a virtue out of circumstance. Any rhetoric about a new politics was merely, therefore, giving cover to party interest.[1]

But this depends on whether we see expedience as something to be always abhorred. It is easy to portray politicians as cynical and seeking to attain power at almost any cost. Yet after the election in May 2010 politicians were left with a situation in which the electorate had spoken, but seemingly without reaching any conclusion. The electorate was not prepared to endorse one party, and then sat in front of their televisions and waited for a government to emerge. The politicians, therefore, had no real alternative but to try to put a government together based on the hand they were dealt. In this sense, Cameron and Clegg had to be expedient and to be any other would have been to deny any purpose for them in politics.

But this apparently expedient rush to create a 'new politics', to make a virtue out of circumstances, raises a more fundamental issue about the Conservatives that is particularly relevant for our study. The Conservatives historically have taken great pride in their flexibility and pragmatism. What matters is being in power and so able to govern (Ramsden, 1998). Cameron has himself declared that he takes a non-ideological view of politics (Jones, 2008). He is not driven by a particular dogma, but by a more general sense of duty and responsibility. So we might suggest that ideas do not form a large part of the Conservative party agenda, and this allowed them readily to accept the possibility of coalition. But this raises a number of questions. Do the Conservatives have a coherent, consistent and well-developed plan for government? And if so, are these new or well-established and well-accepted Conservative views? Did Cameron have a vision for government based on principles, or has his journey from the leadership election in 2005 to power in 2010 been about positioning based on what is expedient?

Cameron has been quick to brand his form of Conservatism as progressive and even liberal. He wishes to see his leadership as a definitive break with the past and this is shown in his rhetoric and the choice of issues he has promoted, such as climate change and civil partnerships (Bale, 2010). However, the expedient manner in which he sought and achieved a coalition, being prepared to compromise and forgo key policy issues, indicates that he is fully a part of the traditional pragmatism and flexibility of the Conservative party.

The really important issue, therefore, is whether Cameron is actually presenting a new politics, or is it just the 'same old Tories'? Is Cameron merely offering a return to the Thatcherism of the 1980s, or perhaps even a return to an older form of Tory paternalism associated with the likes of Macmillan in the 1950s? Cameron's government will inevitably be one that cuts back on public expenditure – the circumstances allow them no choice in the matter – and so their opponents on the left will no doubt suggest that this is merely Thatcherism reborn.[2] In the next chapter we shall look in more detail at the similarities and differences between Thatcher and Cameron. However, the more immediate task is to look at how Cameron arrived at his place at the head of a coalition government. Much of this chapter will be on the 2010 election and its immediate aftermath, but in order to get there we need to consider, albeit briefly, some of the history of the Conservative party from 1992 onwards. It is not my aim here to provide an exhaustive history of the last 20 years of Conservative politics, but really just to pick out what I consider are some of the more salient points that allow us to assess the significance of Cameron's new politics.

1992 and all that

John Major won the 1992 election despite the clear expectation that he would lose (Bale, 2010). The opinion polls pointed to an outright Labour win and even the exit polls on the night of the election did not point to anything but a Conservative defeat (Williams, 1998). They were wrong and Major was returned albeit with a much reduced majority. However, Bale (2010) argues that this victory might in hindsight be seen as a disaster for the party. It did mean that it had five more years in power, but these years were turbulent and did severe damage to the reputation and image of the Conservative party. Within a few months of the election in 1992 the Major government had to deal with a sterling crisis and the ejection of the pound from the Exchange Rate Mechanism (ERM). This destroyed the Conservatives' reputation for economic competence, which had been the very thing on which they had built their long period of electoral success. Bale (2010) suggests that were the Conservatives to have lost the 1992 election, dealing with the crisis then would have fallen to Labour (who in opposition had concurred with the Conservatives' policy on the ERM). This might have allowed the Conservatives to renew themselves quickly in opposition and return to power as early as 1997. In addition, it would not have allowed some of the key fault lines to develop after 1992, particularly with regard to Europe.

So, perhaps somewhat perversely, the 1992 election victory allowed for problems to develop in a way that caused long-term damage to the party. The first point to appreciate is that, while Major achieved a majority, it was a very much reduced one compared to Mrs Thatcher's landslides in 1983 and 1987. This meant that Major was nowhere as secure as his predecessor and found he could not necessarily rely on his backbenchers, again particularly on the issue of Europe.

Indeed, Europe proved to be the most significant fault line, leading to major legislative measures passing through the Commons only by a vote of confidence in the government, the withdrawing of the whip from a number of rebel MPs and a 'clear the air' leadership election in 1995 (Williams, 1998; Bale, 2010). This latter event, where Major resigned as leader of the party and dared his opponents to challenge him, showed how insular the Conservatives had become, seeming to be more concerned with their own internal debates than running the country.

One key issue that heightened this division was the belief that Mrs Thatcher had been unfairly treated when she resigned as party leader in 1991. Many of the MPs newly elected in 1983 and 1987 were overtly Thatcherite in their views, and once the current leadership hit difficulties, it became all too easy to focus the problem on the loss of the great leader. This sense of betrayal, Bale (2010) argues, only grew as the party's woes lengthened. The result was an increasing hardening of attitudes, where a number of so-called 'true believers' started to cause trouble for Major and the leadership. Partly this was over Europe, but it also focused on the formation of the Nolan Committee on Standards in Public Life, which Major set up in 1995 in response to a number of financial and personal scandals affecting the behaviour of (mainly) Conservative MPs.

So the party was becoming more extreme at the same time as it was increasingly disillusioned with the leadership. Much of this might be put down to the effect of what was in historical terms a rather long period of continuous office. The Conservatives had won four elections in succession, winning the last one against expectations. If the Labour party could not win in 2002, the argument went, then it could never win, and so the Conservatives could settle down to almost permanent power (Bale, 2010). Not surprisingly, therefore, what became important to many Conservatives was what was happening within the party rather than outside it.

But there was a further problem that Bale (2010) points to. He suggests that the Conservatives believed that they had convincingly won the battle of ideas. They had comprehensively defeated socialism and that this was a permanent and complete victory. The public, they believed, were on their side of the argument and actually held the same convictions as they did. But this, Bale suggests, was to ignore the real situation that pertained in the 1980s and 1990s. Thatcher may have won three elections convincingly, but she did so against a thoroughly divided opposition and without securing the support of the majority of voters. The split in the Labour party in the early 1980s was an important factor in the Conservatives' continued success.

But secondly, Bale argues that the Conservatives were wrong in assuming that the electorate was as ideological as they were. They mistook electoral support for ideological conviction, and so misjudged the level of positive support they had. This, of course, became more of an issue once the Labour party had healed its splits and elected a young charismatic leader who accepted much of the Thatcherite legacy. But, because of this belief in their connection with the electorate, the Conservatives persistently underestimated Tony Blair and how far the Labour party had changed. The Conservatives seemed to feel that all they needed to do was to be heard and then to expose Blair for the charlatan they believed him to be. What they apparently could not grasp was that the electorate was more than happy to bank the benefits of the Thatcher years, but then look to see what they might be offered elsewhere. In other words, the electorate was much more pragmatic than the Conservatives imagined them to be.

The result of this heightened sense of ideological zeal was some sense that it was better to be right in opposition than wrong in government. It was more important to be right on issues like Europe than it was to be in power doing the wrong things. This might be one explanation of why the Conservatives elected a series of leaders between 1997 and 2003 who proved to be unpopular with the general public. Leaders such as William Hague (1997–2001), Iain Duncan Smith (2001–03) and Michael Howard (2003–05) seemed to have been chosen for who they were not and for what they represented rather than whether they were particularly electable as a prime minister. The party chose not to elect popular and experienced politicians such as Ken Clarke, choosing instead ones who could be trusted ideologically on issues like Europe (Williams, 1998). The result was a party that found itself increasingly out of step with how the country had developed since the 1980s.

Bale (2010) portrays the period between 1997 and 2005 as one where the Conservatives consistently refused to accept that the country had changed and that the agenda of the 1980s and early 1990s no longer pertained. The country did not want more of the same. The result, as Snowdon (2010) points out, was a party seemingly heading for destruction, unable to make any real headway in three successive general elections. Leaders were chosen for the wrong reason and the belief was persisted with that sooner of later the electorate could be persuaded to come back home. But because of the splits over issues like Europe and the call to modernise, particularly on social policy, no leader was able to control the party and create a consensus around a shared agenda (Bale, 2010).

But this situation was compounded by two further factors. First, was the undoubted popularity and apparent effectiveness of Tony Blair and New Labour. Blair was careful to keep what was liked from the Conservative's agenda – privatisation, the sale of council houses, restrictive trade union laws – while adding a different rhetoric that was somehow more glamorous yet more caring and compassionate. The Conservatives waited for the shine to fade from Blair, but it took an awful long time to occur, with perhaps the decisive event being the invasion of Iraq in 2003 (which was anyway supported by the Conservatives and so they were limited in what political capital they had to exploit the government's difficulties).

The second factor – and this doubtless helped Blair to retain his popularity – was the benign economic conditions of the 1990s and beyond. The UK saw continuous economic growth between 1993 and 2007, and while the seeds for this were planted by John Major's government, the fruits were definitely distributed, and with the requisite fanfare, by their successors. It was difficult for the Conservatives, themselves tainted by the ERM debacle, to be critical of Blair's economic record, just as it was hard for them to criticise the extra spending on schools and hospitals provided by the apparently prudent Chancellor, Gordon Brown.

The Conservatives, therefore, were unable to accept that Britain had changed and that they must do the same if they were to return to power. Their problem was that many of these changes were not perhaps readily perceptible, but only became important once a critical mass had been reached. Many of the changes were demographic and generational, especially those relating to personal morality, sexuality and race. What came to bear eventually was a change of attitudes and perceptions as the more relaxed attitudes of the younger generation toward race and sexuality became more widespread. What changed in 1997 was not then a sudden shift in attitudes but rather that there were now politicians such as Blair who seemed to be part of this generation.

Blair was able to accept this more multicultural and permissive view of the world, while many Conservatives still could not. The problem with the Conservatives was their tardiness in accepting these changes or, perhaps more significantly, in proving convincingly that they had accepted them. The Conservatives, it appeared, had stood still and were merely resisting, forgetting that the only way to preserve what is important is to manage the process of change not turn one's back on it. The Conservatives had seemingly lost the ability to react. What was needed was a leader who could tap into Britain as it was, or perceived itself to be, rather than how politicians thought it should be.

The ascent of Cameron

This situation was finally recognised after the election defeat of 2005. Bale (2010) states that many modernisers in the party saw the 2005 election campaign as a whinge against modern Britain, as if the Conservatives resented how the country was changing. This was mirrored by more traditional figures in the party such as Michael (soon to be Lord) Ashcroft, a former party Treasurer and future Vice-Chairman, who used his own money to fund post-election research on what had gone wrong and what the Conservatives needed to do in order to win over the electorate (Bale, 2010). Ashcroft found that many of the Conservatives' arguments on issues like Europe and immigration appealed to less affluent and less educated voters, who either continued to vote Labour or not vote at all, but that the same arguments put off more affluent and better-educated voters. In addition, he found that many non-Conservative voters perceived the party as being hostile to the NHS and public services in general. Ashcroft concluded that little would change for the Conservatives unless and until they changed their image with the broader electorate. What was needed was a 're-branding' of the party (Bale, 2010).

This was precisely what David Cameron set about doing after he was elected leader in December 2005. The most noticeable change was in terms of perspective. He deliberately downplayed the traditional Conservative policies on Europe, immigration and low taxation in favour of a range of softer lifestyle issues. He showed a commitment to dealing with climate change, most famously by visiting the Arctic and being photographed hugging a husky. In his first conference speech as party leader in 2006 he offered what might have sounded like traditional support for families but added that this support should include relationships between gays and lesbians as well heterosexual couples (Bale, 2010). Furthermore, instead of promising to reduce taxation Cameron and his shadow chancellor, George Osbourne, promised merely to share the proceeds of growth.

Cameron also made explicit his support for the NHS, seeing this as one of the key areas the Conservatives needed to shift voters' perceptions. As the parent of a severely disabled child Cameron needed to do little to show his sincerity here. More controversially, he held firm in support of David Willetts, his education spokesperson, in a dispute over Conservative support for grammar schools. Willetts had suggested that the Conservatives would not support the creation of any more grammars, much to the disapproval of elements on the right of the party and in the press. However, Cameron made it clear that he would not move on this issue, despite it being apparent that many in his party did not agree with him (Bale, 2010). There was a sense, which of course Cameron was keen to deny (Jones, 2008), that he was deliberately creating disputes with elements of his party to show how things had changed, just as Blair used the repeal of clause four of the Labour party constitution as a means of showing how his party had changed (Blair, 2010). Katwala (2006) argued that Cameron needed to find safe targets to attack to show the Conservatives were not the nasty right-wing party of old and did this by explicitly attacking and denigrating certain right-wing figures such as the *Daily Telegraph* journalist, Simon Heffer. It was as if Cameron was prepared to rile the old right as a means of making it clear that he had modernised the party and left the old guard behind. Another part of this was making it known that he did not necessarily consider himself the successor of Thatcher but rather was the heir to Blair.

This strategy proved successful in that the Conservatives after 2005 held consistent leads in the opinion polls over Labour, a trend only dented temporarily when Gordon Brown succeeded Blair in the summer of 2007. Indeed, the match up between Cameron and Brown seemed to be much more in the former's favour.

However, this optimistic approach and clear progress to an election victory was dramatically challenged by the onset of the global financial crisis in 2008. The collapse of Northern Rock in the UK and Lehman Brothers in the USA altered not just the economic climate but also that of politics too. It was all very well to suggest that they would share the proceeds of growth, but when the country was in recession the Conservatives' plan looked somewhat absurd. The problem for Cameron and the Conservatives was that they needed to shift from a strategy based on optimism and economic security to recession and austerity. This they were never fully able to do and went into the General Election in May 2010 with slipping ratings in the opinion polls and without any big idea or coherent electoral strategy.

The 2010 election

Any post-mortem on the 2010 election is necessarily speculative, in that we cannot prove a hypothetical. We might suggest that the tactics of a certain party were flawed and that if it had done something else then a different result would have ensued. For example, if Cameron had not agreed to the televised leaders' debates, then the election might have been a straight fight between Brown and himself with no 'Clegg effect' to complicate matters. It might have been the case that if Labour had replaced Brown with a different leader as some in the party wished, then it may have done well enough to at least hang on as the largest party. It is fascinating to speculate on these 'what ifs' but we cannot state anything definitive. This means that those who are critical of the Conservative election campaign cannot state with any certainty that an alternative strategy would have worked better. One can justifiably argue that the election campaign was unfocused, but this does not mean that any other strategy would necessarily have succeeded. Any strategy would have been equally prey to the unforeseen.

Therefore, the only proper criteria we can use is success or failure, and Cameron is in government and seeking to do much, but by no means all, of what he promised to do in the election campaign. As Prime Minister he is just as powerful as if he had a Conservative majority, and that – purely Conservative – government would still have had to prioritise and compromise on certain issues. It may well be that Cameron is particularly comfortable with the arrangements in this coalition, for reasons we shall discuss below, but he could not have predicted this set of outcomes.

Another problem we need to contend with is that much of the discussion and critique about the coalition immediately after the election had a particular purpose often based on pre-existing attitudes towards Cameron and the changes he has made to his party. Those who supported Cameron saw sense in the coalition and argued for its longevity, but those who opposed him were inclined to see it as doomed or unprincipled. We need to see these comments about why Cameron went for a coalition, whether it would last and what effect it would have, in these terms. And, of course, this too is speculation: how can anyone really know how long it will last until they gain the benefit of hindsight?

But first, we need to look at some aspects of the election campaign itself. The Conservative election manifesto (Conservative Party, 2010a) was in some respects a surprise in that it presented a radical idea that was seen as something of a gamble. The format and presentation of the manifesto was commented on favourably, but the contents were also seen by some commentators as a radical departure (Nelson and Forsyth, 2010). The manifesto launched the idea of the Big Society, an attempt to emphasise notions of community, voluntary action and citizen engagement. It sought to differentiate society from the state, and encourage greater public participation and decentralisation.

We shall consider the contents of the manifesto in more detail in Chapter Five, and will now only concern ourselves with its impact. This impact, it is fair to say, was fairly minimal. As Nelson and Forsyth (2010) argue, less than two weeks into the campaign the idea of the Big Society had effectively been dropped. They state that Cameron failed to mention the concept at all in the first televised debate, and once the effect of the debates became clear any ideas took second place to a personality contest between the three main party leaders. Having said that, the Big Society has become increasingly important in the rhetoric and actions of the coalition since the election.

The problem with the Big Society idea in April/May 2010, as Nelson and Forsyth (2010) argue, was that it was launched much too late, only a month before the election. It would have been more sensible for an idea such as this, which could not be reduced to a simple statement without some explanation of what it actually meant, to have been outlined at least two years before an election, leaving the campaign free to specify simple and clear policies based on these principles. But because it was launched so late the full import of the idea could not be explained properly, and it was quickly dropped as events sped away from the Conservatives. An election is a period for putting the flesh on conceptual bones, but the Conservatives were only just at the stage of building the skeleton. This approach, as we shall discover in Chapter Five, was in sharp contrast to the Thatcher period. Their key pre-election document was published as early as 1976, which gave them something to build on during the 1979 campaign. Cameron left no such time to create any solidity for his message, or to explain what it meant in terms of policy.

It was also interesting that during the election the Conservatives did not use the word 'progressive' over much. Any sense of radicalism was downplayed and as the election went on it became ever harder to state what particular message the Conservatives were peddling. Their campaign had little consistency, except for making sure that difficult issues like immigration and the deficit were sidelined. They seemed unable or unwilling to put forward a clear narrative other than being against five more years of Gordon Brown and that a vote for the Liberal Democrats would in effect be a vote for Labour. Theirs was a campaign that had no repeated and repeatable slogan. It was as if they had expected to win and would do so simply by focusing negatively on their opponents. Perhaps the belief was that Gordon Brown was so unpopular and so lacking in charisma that he would effectively hand the election to the Conservatives.

The Conservatives seemed to want to keep commitments to a minimum and not take any risks. This might have been a policy formed for another set of conditions where there was a clear distinction between an unpopular government and a popular opposition. However, events had conspired against this scenario, even if the Conservatives seemed not to fully appreciate this. First, we can suggest the effect of the parliamentary expenses scandal in 2009 impacted equally on all politicians and all parties, so that the Conservatives were just as tarnished as the government. The voters did not merely distrust the Labour government, but all politicians. Second, the impact of the televised debates, which treated Nick Clegg as an equal, hugely complicated the message for the Conservatives. There was an extra element introduced that could not be readily accounted for by a narrative of 'no more Brown'.

Cameron had seen the televised debates as a means of outshining Brown. But once they had been agreed to, it was impossible to deny equal access to Clegg. This, according to critics like Tim Montgomerie (2010), was a huge miscalculation on the part of Cameron and his advisors. With three people participating in the debates, all with equal billing, there could be no simple comparison between Brown and Cameron. Clegg's presence complicated the dynamics of the debates and made them much more unpredictable.

However, there was a more fundamental problem with the debates, which relates to the more long-term strategy adopted by Cameron. Since 2005 he had been portrayed as the 'change candidate'. This approach, as we discussed in the introduction, was not based on specific changes, but merely on the idea of change itself. Cameron's approach was that he was for change, but often without specifying just what he wanted to change. This was a strategy that could work only so long as there was no new candidate to challenge his change credentials. Accordingly, once a new 'change' candidate arrived in the form of Clegg, Cameron was left with little to offer. If change is seen as an end in itself then the newest proposal will often have the most appeal.

Change, as proposed by the Conservatives, was effectively reduced to 'Not-Brown'. But then Clegg arrived on the scene, relatively unknown and unsullied, and electrified the election by declaring he offered a change from both of the old parties. Cameron was left with few options now but to stress his personality and to attack the Liberal Democrats as potentially letting Labour in through the back door.

So the Conservative election can be characterised by a lack of clarity and no clearly understood principles, which meant that it could be easily blown off course by events. Some of these events might have been avoided, such as by refusing to participate in televised debates. However, others like the impact of the financial crisis and the MPs' expenses scandal were outside of the party leadership's control. The result was that the Conservatives won only 307 seats in the House Commons, an increase of 97 but short of the 326 needed to form a majority. The Labour party lost 91 seats but still managed to retain 258, while the Liberal Democrats actually lost 5 seats to finish on 57. The minority parties had 28 seats combined (BBC, 2010). The 'Clegg effect' proved to be an illusion and what actually prevented Cameron attaining a majority was the resilience of Labour in some of its supposedly vulnerable marginal seats.

This inconclusive result led to a frenzied weekend of negotiations, rumour and media speculation about what form of government would emerge. Cameron had announced on the day after the election that he would seek the support of the Liberal Democrats, and talks between the two parties took place over a five-day period. At the same time, Gordon Brown remained as Prime Minister, as the constitutional proprieties dictated, and Labour too sought an arrangement with the Liberal Democrats and perhaps the minority parties to form what they termed a 'progressive alliance' to keep the Conservatives out. However, this proved fruitless, and on 11 May Brown resigned and Cameron entered Downing Street as Prime Minister.

The speculation over what form of government would be formed, however, did not prevent a debate from starting on why the Conservatives were unable to win outright. As we have seen, Montgomerie (2010) argued that there were serious problems with the campaign, especially the lack of policy focus and the agreement to the televised debates, leading to the loss of a once in a generation opportunity to form a majority Conservative government. A more strident criticism of the coalition was presented by Simon Heffer. In a series of articles in the *Daily Telegraph* he criticised the strategy of the Conservatives as being unprincipled (Heffer, 2010a), that Cameron was seeking to demonise the right of the party (Heffer, 2010b) and that the coalition was a betrayal of the Conservative party and was not what millions of voters thought they were voting for (Heffer, 2010c). For all these reasons, Heffer argued, the coalition would fail and deserved to. Heffer, of course, was a long-term critic of Cameron and his modernisation project, but he was certainly not the only commentator to condemn the Conservatives for their failure to win a majority and their subsequent decision to form a coalition. For example, Stephen Glover writing in the *Daily Mail* argued that the Conservative campaign lacked clarity and seemed afraid to stress core issues such as immigration (Glover, 2010). A more dispassionate, but no less critical, view was taken by Anthony King (2010a), again in the *Daily Mail*, who concurred that the Conservatives lacked clarity, and went on to suggest that many voters were left with no clear idea what they would get if they voted for the Conservatives. He thought that the Conservatives did not present a sufficiently clear and inviting vision that could override the voters' sense of disillusion following the MPs' expenses scandal.

Yet, for all the faults of the campaign, the Conservatives were able to move into government and Cameron became Prime Minister. Despite criticism from journalists and party members, the Conservative leadership felt that they had no alternative but to create a new politics and form a coalition. But how new was this politics, and was it really a betrayal of Conservatism?

The coalition

It is perfectly proper and appropriate for the supporters of a political party to argue that what matters is not only winning elections, but what they believe in and promote in the attempt at winning power. What matters are principles, even if this means they fail to win. They have kept their principles and their honour intact, and they have not compromised what they believe in. Of course, this was precisely the view that Bale (2010) suggests had prevailed in the Conservative party in the period between 1992 and 2005. It appears, therefore, that Cameron has not completely succeeded in winning over all elements of Conservative opinion.

But is it really the case that Cameron had betrayed the principles of the Conservative party by forming a coalition? Is it not possible to argue that we can alter the way we take forward our principles according to the circumstances that we face? Is it always unprincipled or inconsistent to form a coalition? Might it not actually be that Cameron had acted in the way that any rational conservative would?

The first issue to consider is what alternative the Conservatives had. They could have sought to form a minority government, but this would have been unstable and might have led to an early General Election which neither the Conservatives nor any of the other parties had any appetite for. In addition, the Conservatives might have thought that they could not seriously attack the deficit and deal with the financial crisis without a clear majority in Parliament. Alternatively, the Conservatives might have stood back and allowed Labour to try to form a coalition of their own. But, this would have been dangerous for the Conservatives, particularly as Labour had promised the Liberal Democrats a referendum on proportional representation. This risked locking the Conservatives out of power virtually indefinitely. Compared to these two options a coalition with the Liberal Democrats, with the Conservatives as the dominant partner, was clearly to be favoured. While it was not without its risks – they too had to promise the possibility of some form of electoral reform to the Liberal Democrats – it potentially offered greater stability than any other option.

But there might be a more subtle reason for Cameron's choice of a coalition. John Curtice (2010) in a post-election review of electoral trends and arithmetic shows that there has been a considerable slump since the 1960s in the support for the two main political parties. Instead of 90–95% support in the early postwar period, it fell to around 65% in 2005 (with Labour obtaining a majority on only 35%), and stayed at this level again in 2010. Voters are more fickle in their allegiance and the various countries and regions of the UK are becoming more polarised to the extent that both Labour and the Conservatives are largely unrepresented in certain parts of the country. This means it is now increasingly difficult for any party to get over 40% of the vote. Accordingly, Curtice argues that it might be necessary to rethink electoral politics and see 35–37% as an optimal outcome.

So what if Cameron and his advisors calculated that 36% was actually the highest figure the Conservatives could expect in the less tribal times of 21st-century Britain? Perhaps, then, the 2010 result was actually about as good as could be expected. There was, therefore, no point in a minority government and another election in late 2010 or 2011 if there was no real prospect of a much improved outcome for the Conservatives.

Of course, some have seen Cameron's calculation as more cynical and driven by a desire to neuter the right of his party. This is the view of Heffer (2010b, 2010c), but he is not alone in this. Philip Stephens (2010) states that some senior Conservatives 'believe the Tory leader might actually be more comfortable governing with Mr Clegg's support than being held to ransom by the more reactionary elements of his own party' (p 3). With the Liberal Democrats on the government benches, Cameron has a majority of over 80 and he can use the Liberal Democrats, who are clearly on the left side of the coalition, to offset the influence of the right on issues such as taxation and Europe. We might argue, therefore, that the coalition government is rather more liberal and metropolitan than a majority Conservative one would have been.

So it might appear that Cameron has actually benefited from the inconclusive outcome of the 2010 election. Even though he does not have a Conservative majority he is the leader of a government with a majority of 80 that commands the implicit support of 60% of the electorate, which allows him cover for his progressive agenda as well as for making the cuts in public spending he and his senior colleagues have deemed necessary. He is actually, therefore, in a much stronger position than if he had received the 38–40% he might have realistically planned for before the election and the rather small majority this would have delivered for his party.

This particular outcome clearly could not have been predicted, and the coalition arose out of expediency, but if it works it might allow him much greater freedom to pursue his avowed agenda of progressive Conservatism. It would be a mistake to see this as part of any master plan, but it might be said to fit in with Cameron's intentions to remake the Conservatives into a progressive party. The coalition gives him the possibility of doing this without him having to take on his right wing immediately, or perhaps even at all.

What Cameron demonstrated was a considerable degree of pragmatism in reacting to a particular set of circumstances. He took an opportunity and used it to a manufacture the most beneficial outcome. This, according to our previous discussion, is an entirely conservative thing to have done and is consistent with the model of pragmatic reaction we have sought to develop.

One issue that has created some speculation, from supporters and critics alike, is how far Cameron would put his party before his government. Heffer (2010b) accused him of betrayal, but is the preservation of the Conservative party more important than the government of the country? Without the Conservative party Cameron would have no vehicle to seek support and win elections. But now he is the leader of a government, Cameron has a different focus: indeed, we might say that he is the focus. The government gives him power and the ability to shape the agenda and so perhaps create the conditions for future success, both personally and for his party. The fact that Cameron is now Prime Minister alters the nature of the gamble that he has taken.

He can shape the agenda; he makes the news and so he is in a position to change the terms in which politics is made. The longer he remains as Prime Minister the stronger his personal position becomes in this regard, and the weaker is that of his critics.

But just how Conservative is the coalition? On one level, of course, only time will tell. However, as this is the only form of Conservatism on offer, we might simply state that it will inevitably be Conservative. But such a statement is not especially helpful, and so we should perhaps rather ask how conservative, with a small 'c', the coalition might be. It will indeed be different because of Liberal Democrat involvement, and we shall consider this more fully in the next section. But, despite the five Liberal Democrats in the Cabinet, Conservatives hold the high offices of state and dominate in terms of numbers, and many of the policies the Conservatives proposed in the election campaign have been retained.

In more general terms, we might suggest that a coalition is not necessarily contrary to a Burkean view of conservatism that we encountered in the introduction. The forming of the coalition, we might suggest, is an example of pragmatism, of a party focusing on the surface of things and on the world as it is. The Conservatives, and the Liberal Democrats, have been expedient and have both acted in an entirely practical manner, rather than according to rigid and abstract principles. We might even say that Cameron has preserved what is important by taking the least worst option, and so ensured that the Conservative way of politics has been maintained, for the moment at least. He has actively tried to turn the 'least worst' into something positive and lasting.

The coalition shows the contingent nature of politics and the need to react expediently as the situation demands. It is, interestingly, exactly how all the parties reacted after the election: the Liberal Democrats sought the best deal for themselves after a good campaign but a poor result; Labour tried to engineer a so-called 'progressive coalition' in order to cling to power and keep the Tories out; and the Conservatives did what they needed to do to form a government that allowed them to pursue as much of their agenda as possible. What favoured the Liberal Democrats and the Conservatives, and handicapped Labour, were the specific circumstances that pertained after the election. This suggests that we can see the coalition as both Conservative and conservative: it is dominated by the Conservative party, but also represents a conservative vision of pragmatic and reactive governance. We might suggest that while some critics could argue that Cameron is not always a Conservative he remains a practical conservative in the manner that he reacts to events.

The influence of the Liberal Democrats

A coalition needs more than one partner and so we need to look at the Liberal Democrats to see what part they have and might play in the new politics. Nick Clegg, the Liberal Democrat leader, made great play of the fact that his party was different from what he referred to as the 'old parties'. However, the Liberal Democrats, or at least one their founder parties, the Liberals, have a history at least as long as the Conservatives and are much older than Labour (Dutton, 2004).

Since the Labour party moved to the right after the election of Tony Blair as leader in 1994, the Liberal Democrats increasingly saw themselves as the most leftwing of the mainstream parties. This view only became more manifest with their opposition to the Iraq War in 2003. In the 2010 election they argued for an extension of civil liberties, but also opposed university tuition fees and the renewal of the Trident nuclear missile defence system. Unlike the Conservatives they showed ambivalence toward the USA and were in favour of Britain joining the Euro (Liberal Democrats, 2010). However, we should also note that many of the leadership of the party, including Nick Clegg, had associated themselves with the so-called 'Orange Book' tendency that sought to introduce a more free-market economic strain into Liberal Democrat thinking (Marshall and Laws, 2004).

As we have seen, Clegg was very much the star of the election campaign and there was an expectation towards the end of the campaign that the Liberal Democrats might push Labour into third place in terms of vote share if not in the number of seats. However, the result of the election did not bear this out, and even though the Liberal Democrats achieved a marginally higher share of the vote compared to 2005, they actually lost five seats. However, because of the distribution of seats after the election, they were able to influence the formation of the next government to perhaps a greater extent than had been thought possible even at the height of so-called 'Cleggmania'.

This effect is not only in the personnel of the government, but on its policies as well. The coalition had not taken on the Conservatives' plans to reduce Inheritance Tax and to offer tax breaks to encourage marriage,[3] and instead adopted a Liberal Democrat policy of increasing personal allowances for the lowest paid. This shift in tax policy, while it goes against key parts of the Conservative manifesto, strengthens the coalition's claim that it is putting fairness and progress at the heart of its programme.

But the Liberal Democrats also allow Cameron to present a more coherent national strategy to the country, particularly with regard to dealing with the deficit. The Liberal Democrats are tied into the strategy of public sector cuts, and the combined vote share of nearly 60% allows for a solid platform. The government can claim that, in a time of national emergency, it is not promoting the agenda of just one party that only gained a minority of support in the country. Rather it rests on a clear majority of voters and can justly claim a broad basis for its policies. In addition, as I have already suggested, the presence of 57 Liberal Democrats can act as a counterweight to the right wing of the Conservative party and so allow Cameron some leeway in pursuing his agenda.

While there was much discussion about the stability of the coalition, some of which centred on how far the Liberal Democrats would stomach voting for Conservative policies, it might also be the case that having Liberal Democrats in the government might actually create greater stability. Partly this is for the reasons mentioned above – a broader base and a counterweight to the right – but also because having gone into coalition, the Liberal Democrats have a clear interest in maintaining it. They are the ones who have come under attack for an apparent lack of principle in joining with the Conservatives, and who may suffer as a result at any subsequent election. This has indeed been the outcome of Conservative–Liberal coalitions in the past (Ramsden, 1998). If they do become unpopular then they have a clear interest in maintaining the coalition for as long as possible.

But there are also some positive reasons for the Liberal Democrats preserving the coalition. Prior to the election campaign, for a Liberal Democrat to suggest that they would be in government would have been seen as the very height of wishful thinking. It was not something to be taken seriously for a party, operating in a first-past-the-post system of elections, which had regularly received only about 20% of the vote. The particular set of circumstances that arose out of the 2010 election has given the Liberal Democrats an unanticipated opportunity to be in government, and indeed we might suggest that it is only through a coalition that they can expect to be there again. Therefore maintaining the coalition is their only hope of maintaining a foothold in government. In addition, the Liberal Democrats need the coalition to last for some time into the future to ensure that they can achieve their more long-term aims of political and electoral reform.

Lastly, a sustained period in government will have a marked impact on how the Liberal Democrats are perceived. Clearly, they will not be able to claim that they are outsiders seeking the protest vote against the major parties. But to balance this they will become seen as a party of government and senior Liberal Democrat politicians will become seen as more substantial and important political figures. Instead of being relatively unknown outsiders they are now serious politicians running government departments. This can only have a positive impact on how they are perceived by the electorate. It is therefore clearly in the interest of the Liberal Democrats to maintain and support the coalition. This does not mean that the coalition will last for its full five-year term. However, these circumstances are the most stable outcome that could be expected from the inconclusive result of the 2010 election.

What is interesting is that since the formation of the coalition, the Liberal Democrats have themselves been forced to compromise their previously held positions in the face of the reality of government. In October 2010, the Business Secretary, Vince Cable, despite pledging to oppose university tuition fees before the election, accepted the main recommendations of a report on the future funding of higher education. This involved increasing fees from just over £3,000 to £9,000 per annum. The responsibility of making decisions in constrained circumstances meant that the Liberal Democrats in the coalition had no alternative to changing their position. So perhaps we should conclude that conservative pragmatism is rather widespread, and might even be a condition of sensible government.

A policy example: welfare reform

In the final section of this chapter I wish to look at just one example of the coalition government's programme to assess whether it does represent a new politics. There are two immediate problems in attempting to do this. First, there is the problem of selection: which, if any, policy is most representative of the coalition? We might choose their policy on international development and so stress compassion and internationalism, or we might point to defence policy, which is more hard-headed, but also an area where the coalition agreement allows the Liberal Democrats to abstain (Cabinet Office, 2010). Clearly, therefore, the very choice of policy area will skew the discussion. Therefore, I have chosen an area of policy – welfare reform – where the two parties are in apparent agreement but which is central to both reform and dealing with the budget deficit.

The second issue is that, at the time of writing (October 2010), the coalition is only just laying out its long-term plans for government, following the party conferences and the Comprehensive Spending Review (CSR) in October 2010.

This means that we are restricted to talking about what the coalition plans to do rather than what it has actually achieved. But again welfare reform is an appropriate choice in that this is one area that is relatively well developed. Therefore, looking at welfare reform seems to be a suitable area to look at what is new about the politics of the coalition.

Welfare reform falls within the area of the Department for Work and Pensions (DWP), and consistent with coalition practice, the departmental ministers are from both the Conservatives and the Liberal Democrats. Indeed the team chosen for the DWP was particularly strong, consisting of ministers with a strong track record in the area of welfare policy. The Secretary of State is Iain Duncan Smith, who after his less than successful period as Conservative leader between 2001 and 2003 had re-invented himself through the work of the think tank he established called the Centre for Social Justice (CSJ). The CSJ had produced a series of reports on the state of welfare in Britain, including *Breakthrough Britain* (CSJ, 2007), a document in excess of 600 pages detailing policy recommendations on educational failure, economic dependency and worklessness, family breakdown, addiction, personal debt and the third sector. In 2009 the CSJ also produced a detailed study of the benefits system entitled *Dynamic Benefits* (CSJ, 2009), which considers the reform of the welfare system to ensure that economic dependency is minimised and that households are always better off in work than on benefits. These documents, and particularly the latter one, can be said to form the basis for government policy in this area.

The other members of the ministerial team were Chris Grayling, who had been the DWP shadow minister for a period before the election, Lord David Freud, who had written a report on reforming the pension system for the Blair government and subsequently joined the Conservatives and been enobled. Maria Miller, who had shadowed family policy in opposition for the Conservatives, was made Minister for the Disabled. Lastly, the Liberal Democrat Stephen Webb, a former professor of social policy, was appointed. Therefore, the DWP ministerial team was both very strong and brought with it considerable experience. In addition, the government appointed two Labour politicians to offer more independent support: the current MP and former welfare minister, Frank Field, was appointed to review policy on child poverty, and former MP and Secretary of State for Work and Pensions, John Hutton, was asked to look at pension reform. There has, therefore, been a concerted attempt to bring in expertise and experience from all parties in recognition of the fact that welfare reform is both an area of considerable controversy, but also one which inevitably has long-term consequences financially, materially and politically.

While policy is still being formed, a clear direction is being set with the DWP working on the dynamic benefits model proposed by the CSJ (2009). The aim is to make work pay and reduce the numbers of those who choose to remain on benefits. This is to involve some incentives, but it also involves a focus on sanctions and a toughening of the benefits system.

The first example of this came in the Emergency Budget in June 2010, where the government announced plans to cap Housing Benefit payments and implement a 10% reduction for those on Jobseeker's Allowance for more than one year. In addition, a new form of medical assessment was to be introduced for Disabled Living Allowance, paid to those with long-term disabilities and illness, with a view to saving 10% of the cost of this benefit. The government also announced that it would use the consumer price index (CPI) measure of inflation to adjust benefit rates rather than the generally higher retail price index (RPI) measure (HM Treasury, 2010a). These changes were part of an Emergency Budget that was specifically aimed at tackling the public deficit and so were quite limited.

However, the DWP has since developed policy much further. In July 2010 it released a consultation document entitled *21st Century Welfare* (DWP, 2010), which outlined a number of options for welfare reform. It was clear that the preferred option was for a fundamental revision of the benefits system replacing the many existing benefits with a Universal Credit. It became clear in October 2010 that this was to be taken forward by government, despite the upfront costs of implementing the new system. In order to fund this extra expense the coalition announced what might be seen as a fundamental shift in the nature of welfare provision in the UK. From 2013 Child Benefit, a universal benefit paid to mothers to assist with child costs, was to be restricted only to standard-rate taxpayers. This breached the principle of universal benefits whereby all members of society could expect something in return from the welfare state. What was interesting was that the proposed cut to Child Benefit, which affected those with incomes above about £44,000 per annum, caused much more comment and controversy than the announcement that the welfare benefits system would be facing its biggest overhaul in 70 years. However, what it shows is that the coalition, despite arising out of expedience and compromise, is prepared to take controversial and long-term decisions based on clear principles. It might also show that the coalition understood the politics of long-term reform. By making a great public display of the cut to Child Benefit the coalition achieved some cover for its more fundamental reforms of means-tested welfare.

These proposals were fleshed out further in the Comprehensive Spending Review, announced in October 2010 (HM Treasury, 2010b). The Review was perhaps the most significant in determining the plans of the coalition in that it spells out the level of spending – and therefore the cuts that the government intends to make over the life of the Parliament. The savings in discretionary spending amount to a total of £81 billion between 2011 and 2015. This, it was estimated, would lead to the loss of 490,000 public sector jobs over the period. The government argued that:

> The Spending Review makes choices. Particular focus has been given to reducing welfare costs and wasteful spending. This has enabled the Coalition Government to prioritise the NHS, schools, early years provision and the capital investments that support long term economic growth, setting the country on a new path towards long term prosperity and fairness. As a result of these choices, departmental budgets other than health and overseas aid will be cut by an average of 19 per cent over four years, the same as planned by the previous government (HM Treasury, 2010b, p 5)

This suggests that the coalition is taking a particular direction: they are protecting health and overseas aid, as well as spending on schools, science and certain capital projects, but at the expense of other areas such as housing and local government spending with a cut of 33%, higher education with a cut of 40%, and a cut of 23% in departmental administration costs.

But a clear target for spending reduction is the welfare budget, particularly means-tested benefits. The Review confirmed the government's commitment to welfare reform and made an extra allocation of £2 billion to help with the implementation of the Universal Credit. However, further spending reductions were announced particularly relating to further restrictions to Housing Benefit and Employment Support Allowance and Incapacity Benefit. However, the Review committed the government to making no further reductions to universal, non-means-tested benefits for the life of the current Parliament. The cuts proposed are therefore clearly targeted on specific groups, while keeping universal services and benefits relatively intact. They are also intended to have a clear purpose of linking spending reductions to fundamental reforms particularly in the area of welfare benefits and economic dependency.

But it is perfectly possible to see these proposed reforms in a different light. In the Budget debates in June 2010 and the aftermath of the Comprehensive Spending Review, the Labour opposition seemed to alight on two strategies. The first was to challenge the Liberal Democrats for the compromises they made in joining the coalition, particularly with regard to benefits cuts and increases in VAT. But secondly, Labour have suggested that the Budget and Spending Review were merely smokescreens that allows the Conservatives, who are apparently still Thatcherites at heart, to do what they wished to do all along, namely to cut benefits for the poorest in society. These announcements were merely another example of the 'same old Tories', of the Conservative party reverting to type and cutting public spending while also proposing to reduce Corporation Tax for business.

On one level this can be seen as little more than rhetoric from a party whose main purpose is now to oppose the government. Indeed, had Labour won the 2010 election they would have been faced with the same financial situation as the coalition and with the same need to make significant cuts, some of which were already planned and announced before the election. However, the claim of it being just the 'same old Tories' does raise a number of issues that are pertinent to our more general discussion. The first, and perhaps most controversial issue, is whether it matters if these policies are Thatcherite or not. For many on the left the word 'Thatcherite' is taken as a term of abuse, but this is not the case for many, perhaps most, Conservatives. They see no problem in being associated with somebody who they consider to be the greatest peacetime Prime Minister of the 20th century. But, of course, the Liberal Democrats are not so sanguine about being accused of continuing the work of Mrs Thatcher, and the same might apply to some of the modernisers in the Conservative party. It therefore matters more because there is a coalition that seeks to pursue a progressive agenda.

Reforms to public policy in democratic societies can only be made through consent and by increments. Institutions cannot be scrapped or closed for a period while they are fundamentally reformed. Instead change must occur while these institutions are still undertaking their basic functions. Moreover, these institutions operate within a complex and dynamic environment, such that a change in one area can influence many others. As a result we should expect democratic politicians and policy makers to be expedient and opportunistic (but, of course, without ever admitting as much). They can only work within the conditions in which they find themselves. Welfare systems can be reformed only while they still provide services to households, and these reforms have to be engineered according to current economic and political conditions. So the use of the Emergency Budget to start the process of welfare reform is both sensible and rational: indeed what would be the alternative? Likewise, the government plans to implement its more fundamental welfare reforms over an eight-year period to minimise their disruptive effects and the spread the upfront costs.

But also we need to acknowledge that it would be odd indeed if there were no continuity between past and present Conservatives. It is, after all, the same party, and one moreover which has tended to garner much from the past. The Conservative party has been made in large part by its history and the Thatcher legacy is an important element in that, as we have seen in the earlier parts of this chapter. Cameron is reacting to both the Labour governments of Blair and Brown, and to the Thatcher and Major administrations.

What raises the stakes, however, is that the Thatcher period is considered to be so consequential, and this applies to both left and right. Any new Conservative administration was bound to be compared to that of Thatcher, and likewise its opponents would use the link as a means of commenting on and criticising it. This is only more so when that administration is only partly, but not totally, Conservative. If Thatcher is the benchmark, then how does Cameron measure up?

We need to tackle this question head on, and so having opened up the issue of the new politics by looking at how we got to a coalition government, we now need to focus on Cameron's brand of Conservatism more specifically, and how it relates to Conservatism in the past. Therefore, in the next chapter, we consider the plans put forward by Cameron and the coalition and relate them to what Mrs Thatcher's Conservatives proposed in the run up to their election victory in 1979. This will allow us to be more definitive about what is new in the coalition and what is more of a continuation of the traditional form of Conservative governance. A side issue will also be to compare the manner in which Cameron and Thatcher prepared for government and whether this might tell us anything about why Cameron failed to achieve the same initial electoral success as his illustrious predecessor.

Notes

[1] We need to remember that Labour actively sought to put together a coalition even though they would have found it virtually impossible to achieve a Commons majority. What the other two parties did was not, therefore, particularly outrageous.

[2] Opponents of the Conservatives always seem to believe that referring to them as 'Thatcherite' is somehow to be taken as an insult. They forget that Mrs Thatcher was one of the most popular and successful politicians of the 20th century, and that the Left only became electable when it realised this and accepted many of her changes.

[3] Cameron, however, did hint in October 2010 that a tax break for married couples might be forthcoming later in the Parliament.

FIVE

The same old Tories

Introduction

If one reads about the great Conservative leaders of the past one is struck by a number of things. Leaders such as Salisbury (Roberts, 1999) and Balfour (Adams, 2007), who led the party in the late 19th and early 20th centuries, were patricians who took up politics not out of any real sense of ideological ardour, but rather out of a sense of duty. At this point in history, politicians were not paid and the very idea of being so would be seen not just as unnecessary but as absurd by landowning aristocrats such as Salisbury and Balfour. Neither of these leaders became politicians in order to change anything. Instead they reacted to circumstance on the basis of a number of principles and prejudices. They did not see themselves as representing a particular class or interest, although many others did, but rather they saw governing as an end in itself.

We might suggest that politics in the 20th century could not be more different. Politics is now a job, for which people receive a salary.[1] But politicians have more than a salary: they also have a vision, a purpose and a desire to change and reform. Since the 1960s the Conservative party has had a succession of leaders who were rather more classless than Robert Gascoyne-Cecil, 3rd Marquess of Salisbury. Indeed, after a succession of grammar and comprehensive school graduates, it was commonly felt that the days of the Conservative party being led by a grandee were no longer tenable.

However, the Conservative party membership has proven to be rather more open-minded than this commonly held view suggested and in 2005 elected an Eton-educated leader with links into the aristocracy. For many people the background of a political leader did not seem to matter.[2] However, what is interesting is that this new leader, David Cameron, appears to share some of the political characteristics of the great Tory grandees of the past.

While Mrs Thatcher and her legacy is seen as having a decidedly ideological edge, Cameron has suggested that he is not ideologically driven but rather acts from a sense of duty or responsibility (Jones, 2008). He is avowedly pragmatic and makes no claim to being an original thinker. Nor does he see this apparent lack of originality as a problem. This, it seems to me, is entirely of a part with the more traditional, pre-Thatcherite view of Conservatism, which is concerned with action rather more than ideas (Ramsden, 1998). Such Conservatives do not see the need for ideological purity in order to be a successful politician. They certainly have a moral framework and they can articulate this when called upon to do so. But this view is a settled one that needs no further exploration and debate. There are certain received ideas which they accept and these can be expressed in commonly held concepts and reference points such as the idea of the 'little platoons' identified by Burke (1999b), and the notion of civil society. What is important about these concepts, as we have seen in our discussions of thinkers such as Burke and Oakeshott, is that they are grounded in lived experience rather than intellectual abstraction.

The formation of the coalition with the Liberal Democrats makes this pragmatism all the more relevant. Instead of striking out on his own with a minority government and keeping his programme intact, Cameron was prepared to compromise, risk the ire of sections of his party and the press, and seek to form a coalition with what were presumed to be unlikely bedfellows. Of course, this does not suggest he lacked self-interest, or wasn't considering his party's interest either. However, it intimates that what mattered was not ideology but institutions, both parochial and national, and their maintenance.

But this too, as historians such as Adams (2007) and Roberts (1999) remind us, is precisely what the Victorian Tory grandees did. The period from the mid-1880s right up to the 1920s was one where the Conservatives were the dominant part of a coalition with Liberal Unionists. This involved the sharing of key offices in government and compromising over policy. But this was done because the electoral arithmetic dictated such as outcome if the Conservatives were ever to rule.

All this might suggest that Cameron is a throwback to a past generation of Conservative leaders. Yet, as we have seen, he has sought quite deliberately to break with the past and to stress his modernist credentials. He wishes to be seen as a progressive and as a liberal Conservative, something that both Salisbury and Balfour might have found rather eccentric.

What is fascinating is the speculation that Cameron could be both a throw back, or rather a typical Conservative leader, as well as being a moderniser. It might be the case that this is indeed not a contradiction, but actually what all successful Conservative politicians, to some extent or another, have been. They have started from a set of principles, and then adapted these according to circumstance, such that governing becomes a reactive process based on the flow of events. Indeed, might it not be the case that Mrs Thatcher, despite the manner in which she is often portrayed, was equally typical of this form of Conservative leadership? This is the contention that I wish to explore in this chapter, namely that successful Conservatives can appear to offer a new politics while remaining the 'same old Tories'. Moreover, I wish to argue that such as model of pragmatism fits entirely within the conventional view of conservatism I have discussed in Chapter One.

Nelson and Forsyth (2010), in an interview with David Cameron a week before the 2010 election, quote him as stating, with a degree of frustration, that the Big Society is consistent with his message since becoming leader and with the party's past:

> The ideas Mr. Cameron has come out with, such as the Big Society, may well be radical. They are firmly in the Tory tradition. But might these have worked better if it had been wheeled out much earlier, rather than just a month before the election? 'To be fair, I have been wheeling it out for five years,' he says, looking frustrated. But it was only when he introduced the phrase 'Big Society' three weeks ago, he says, that the media started to pay attention to the principle. (p 12)

For Cameron, therefore, he is being radical, but this is not out of step with the history of his party.

This chapter will consist of a comparison between Cameron and Thatcher, and more specifically, the pitches they made in their first election campaigns. I have chosen to do this for two reasons. First, the Thatcher period is often seen as the most ideological, where the Conservatives were least open to compromise, and so there might be some difference between them and the avowedly non-ideological Cameron. What makes this more relevant is that Mrs Thatcher was able to secure a clear majority, while Cameron did not. Second, these two politicians were the last two Conservative Prime Ministers to take over from a Labour government; 1979 and 2010 were the last two occasions when the two main parties switched between government and opposition. This meant that the Conservative party had to put forward a statement of how it would wish to govern, rather than in 1983, 1987 and 1992 where it was merely seeking to stay in power.

So looking at 1979 and 2010 provides us with clear statements of intent. Of course, it does not follow that what a party claimed to do in its election literature is consistent with what actually occurred. However, this is the only comparison possible at this time, it being so soon after Cameron has entered Downing Street. But this choice is not entirely driven by this pragmatic consideration. The materials I look at here are all formal documents, so they tell us what the Conservatives wished the public to know about, and so be judged upon. These are their key public statements, which relate principles to policies and a programme for government. This, we might suggest, is what Conservatism consisted of in both 1979 and 2010.

I wish to consider three key documents relating to the Cameron government: the 2010 Conservative Election Manifesto (Conservative Party, 2010a); the document issued just prior to the election entitled *A Contract Between the Conservative Party and You* (Conservative Party, 2010b) and the Coalition Agreement (Cabinet Office, 2010) issued after the election and once the government had been set up. The purpose of looking at these documents is to search for some sense of what the coalition is about, what they intend to do, and how much of this comes from the Conservative side of the arrangement.

I then wish to compare these with two documents published by the Conservative party in the period prior to the 1979 election. These are: *The Right Approach* (Conservative Party, 1976), a comprehensive statement of policy and principle from 1976; and the 1979 Election Manifesto (Conservative Party, 1979). These documents will allow for a similar consideration of what the Conservatives intended prior to 1979. This will then allow for some assessment of the differences and similarities between the Conservatives at these two points in time when they were expecting, or hoping, to take over from a Labour government and so reorient the country away from what they considered to be failed policies.

Of course, apart from the two manifestos, these documents are not direct correlates. This is simply because such documents do not exist, and we would have no reason to presume they would. However, they do put forward a set of core ideas and a policy framework, and so we might say that they fulfil a similar purpose. We should, therefore, be able to see what connections there are over time and in what ways, if any, Cameron differed from Thatcher.

It is not my aim here to carry out of a formal discourse analysis of these documents. Rather I am seeking to point to areas of continuity and difference that come from the detailed discussion of conservatism, progress and reaction considered in the first part of this book. I have suggested that there are key themes that arise from this discussion and these can be used to assess these otherwise quite different documents.

What I hope will derive from this study is some sense of how seriously we are to take the idea of Cameron's Conservatives as a progressive force and whether they are just the same old Tories their critics might paint them as, and whether this criticism matters.

However, before comparing and contrasting these documents there are a number of rather obvious similarities and differences between Cameron and Thatcher. We need to consider these first, and deal with any issues and problems of analysis that arise from them, before getting to look at the documents. The comparison between the two leaders is, of course, illuminating and interesting of itself, but our main aim is in understanding the nature of contemporary Conservatism and how consistent it is with the history of the party: what we need to do is to understand Cameron in the light of the history of the Conservatives as well as the conservative disposition.

Cameron versus Thatcher

Mrs Thatcher was Prime Minister for 11 years and was the author of many controversial and far-reaching changes (Green, 2006). However, we can see her achievements with hindsight, which allows us to view her legacy as a complete entity, and so we might forget how relatively precarious her position was in the late 1970s and the early 1980s before the Falklands War. If the Labour Prime Minister, James Callaghan, had called and won an election in 1978, or had Labour not chosen such poor leaders and had senior Labour politicians not left to form the Social Democratic Party, then Thatcher's period as Conservative leader might now be seen as a brief aberration. Yet events turned out as they did and we can now only see Thatcher as the dominant politician of the last half of the 20th century.

Cameron can still only be seen as something of a novice in comparison; one who has achieved much, but is as yet untested in government. It is therefore unfair and unreasonable to compare him with Thatcher, apart from, of course, his inability to win a clear majority. Clearly, we cannot as yet judge Cameron in the same light as his predecessor. As yet he has been able to achieve little in government, and so we need to look elsewhere for comparisons with Thatcher. What might be useful is to look at the similarities and differences between the two leaders at the point at which they took office.

There are indeed a number of important similarities between the two leaders. Both were not new leaders by the time they took office. They had both been leader of the Conservatives for more than four years by the time of their first election and so they were reasonably well–established and known quantities. They had been given time to remake the party and fight the election on their own terms.

Both Thatcher and Cameron faced a Labour government that was commonly seen to have failed economically. The Callaghan government had been forced to seek an emergency loan from the International Monetary Fund in 1976, while Brown had built up the largest peacetime public deficit in the country's history. So both new Prime Ministers could claim that they were dealing with a serious economic situation calling for swift and decisive action.

We might suggest that both these leaders were of a distinctly new type when compared to their predecessors. Mrs Thatcher, of course, was the first woman to lead a major party and become Prime Minister, but she was also more economically liberal and radical than any previous Conservative leader in recent times. Likewise, Cameron presented himself as a moderniser seeking to break free of the image of the Conservatives as being somewhat ruthless and only concerned with economics. The appointment of both these leaders was seen as something of a risk for the party, and a considerable part of their pitch to the country was a repudiation of elements of the party's recent past. Both Thatcher and Cameron saw the need for fundamental change within the Conservative party in response to past mistakes and failures. Mrs Thatcher had served in the Heath government, which she saw as being weak and too prone to concede ground and which had lost two elections in 1974 (Green, 2006). Cameron had taken part in two election defeats and seen the party's inability to recognise that the country had moved on (Bale, 2010). So both leaders saw the need for change and set about achieving it.

A final point of similarity is that both leaders are controversial figures within the Conservative party. They sought to drag an often uncomprehending party into a direction they might not have realised they needed to move in. This, as we saw in the previous chapter, has been the cause of some resentment, from the right of the party in Cameron's case. With Thatcher it was the left – or the 'wets' – that objected and sought to resist change (Ramsden, 1998).

These are important points of confluence, but we should also point to a number of important differences. The first is that in 1979 the Conservatives had been out of power only for five years, not 13 as in Cameron's case. Between 1964 and 1979 there had been regular changes at elections and there was no sense in which this would not carry on. Governments expected only small majorities rather than landslides. Of course, Thatcher herself broke with this pattern with her election victories in 1983 and 1987. Cameron, however, became leader after three successive election defeats and with the Conservatives needing to gain over 100 seats just to form a majority. This meant that, even though he achieved a swing almost as big as Thatcher achieved in 1979, he did not achieve the same outcome and hence had to form a coalition. So, the starting points, and expectations, of the two leaders were markedly different: Conservatives of Thatcher's generation could expect to be in power frequently; Cameron's generation could not.

This leads to a second important difference. Many of the 1979 Conservative cabinet, including Thatcher herself, had already gained experience of government office, which is not the case in 2010. Cameron himself had no previous Cabinet experience, having been only a political advisor prior to 1997. Only two members of the 2010 government had previous Cabinet experience – Ken Clarke and William Hague – and so they could be said to be less ready for government than was the case in 1979.[3]

In addition, of course, the Conservatives in 2010 are not ruling on their own. Thatcher was able to win a clear majority for her party. This points to two issues. First, that Cameron has a much lower level of electoral support than Thatcher. Thatcher achieved between 42% and 44% of the vote in each of her three election victories (Ramsden, 1998) compared to the 36% attained in 2010 by Cameron (BBC, 2010). However, Thatcher, at least for her first election victory (which is our point of comparison), was operating within a two-party system, where Labour and the Conservatives could expect to garner over 90% of the vote between them. In 2010 the Conservatives were operating in what was effectively a three-party system, with the Liberal Democrats consistently achieving 20% in elections. Moreover, the major parties are increasingly becoming regional rather than truly national, UK-wide parties (Curtice, 2010). Labour now has scant representation in the South (outside London) and West, while the Conservatives have only one MP in Scotland and have very little presence in the major Northern conurbations. This suggests that it is much harder for the Conservatives to win an election in 2010 than was the case in the 1970s and 1980s.

A further difference that should not be underestimated, even if we cannot yet fully consider its effect, is that Cameron is facing a much larger set of economic and political problems than Thatcher had to deal with. The scale of the public deficit and debt is much greater than in 1979 and the impact is global rather than local. Much of the coalition's energies will have to be spent on deficit reduction and securing economic growth. This does not mean that they will not attempt to make changes elsewhere, and nor should we minimise the controversy caused by Mrs Thatcher's economic policies in the early

1980s. However, it does suggest that the Cameron government will be much more at the mercy of events and external forces than many of its predecessors.

Politicians, we might suggest, have always been held in rather low regard (at least until they retire). However, following the parliamentary expenses scandal in 2009, most politicians, and politics in general, are now held in contempt. This means that voters are sceptical of a politician's intentions and are less prepared to give them the benefit of the doubt.

A final point to consider is the state of the opposition to the government. Mrs Thatcher soon found herself facing a divided opposition, with the major party of opposition shifting to the left and electing leaders who proved unpopular, and then splitting in two. This proved to be very convenient for the Conservatives in the 1980s and helped them to subsequent election victories. Cameron cannot claim such as luxury, at least not yet. In October 2010 the Labour party elected Ed Miliband as leader to replace Gordon Brown. It is not possible at the time of writing to suggest how this might impact on Labour. However, despite a poor performance historically Labour still has over 250 MPs and this gives it a sound basis to build towards the next election. Moreover, as the Liberal Democrats, who have typically been the beneficiary of protest votes, are now part of the coalition, Labour is the sole focus for opposition to the government. This would suggest, all things being equal, that Cameron will face a stronger and more united opposition.

There is a final point we need to consider here, which should warn us that we must treat any comparison with a degree of caution. No politician operates in isolation. They are prey to events and these might be local or global; these events might be caused by errors made by the government or they might be entirely unexpected and come as if from nowhere. It is not possible for these events to be pre-empted or predicted. But also any politician has to act on the basis of what their predecessors have done. So something of what Cameron has already done, and plans to do, has arisen because of Thatcher. Cameron has to react to her legacy, just as he has had to react to the Blair and Brown governments, and the failed leaderships of Hague, Duncan Smith and Howard. Cameron is aware of what Thatcher achieved because she came before him, and so whatever he does is, to a lesser or greater extent, affected by Thatcher. We are, therefore, not conducting anything like a controlled experiment here. Indeed to try and isolate the influence of Thatcher on Cameron would be to completely defeat the point of this exercise.

What Cameron said

The Conservatives under Cameron's leadership published many policy documents on a whole range of issues, from defence to decentralisation, health to housing, and work to welfare. But, unlike the Conservatives in the1970s, they did not bring out an overall statement of their aims and intentions with the purpose of creating a coherent narrative for these policies to slot into. It was not until the election manifesto in 2010 that the Conservatives presented an overall policy statement.

The manifesto (Conservative Party, 2010a) was entitled *Invitation to Join the Government of Britain*, and it certainly caught the attention, garnering both enthusiastic reviews and mocking criticism. In terms of presentation it was indeed distinctive, being unlike the standard 'report form' design that had become standard. Instead it was produced as a small blue hardback, and was full of colourful retro-style graphics. The text, as we shall see below, was written in short sentences, full of abstract nouns. This was a style very much associated with New Labour that might be termed 'Blairite demotic'.

As we would expect, the manifesto was very much a document of its time. We can see this by the particular emphasis placed specifically on green issues, which takes up 13 of the 118 pages. This compares with less than three pages specifically on dealing with the deficit.

The manifesto was certainly aimed to be an eye-catching document and it indeed gained more attention at its launch than those of either Labour or the Liberal Democrats. Part of this, of course, was because the Conservatives were favourites to win the election. But the document was certainly different and distinctive. It was also, as Nelson and Forsyth (2010) pointed out (and as we saw in Chapter Four), a radical departure. It was a conscious attempt to place a big idea before the electorate.

This big idea came across right at the start of the manifesto. The Conservatives sought to present themselves as offering something radically different from what they described as Labour's top-down approach:

> So we offer a new approach: a change not just from one set of politicians to another; from one set of policies to another. It is a change from one political philosophy to another. From the idea that the role of the state is to direct society and micro-manage public services, to the idea that the role of the state is to strengthen society and make public services serve the people who use them. In a simple phrase,

the change we offer is from big government to Big Society.
(Conservative Party, 2010a, p vii)

The Conservatives were offering to create this Big Society, which
they described as an activist, participatory society in which power is
devolved and where citizens take responsibility for services as much
as professionals.

This, the Conservatives suggested, was part of a long-term plan that
started with the election of Cameron as leader in 2005:

> the Party has remoulded itself for the modern era, applying
> its deepest values and beliefs to the urgent problems of
> the hour. Even as it has done so, the problems confronting
> Britain have escalated, and escalated fast. So our ideas are
> ambitious and radical as well as modern. They match the
> scale of Britain's problems, and in tune with a world that
> is changing before our eyes. But our core values have not
> altered and our core beliefs remain consistent. (p vii)

These values and beliefs, it has to be said, are not really spelt out in any
clear manner. However, it is evidently important for the Conservatives
to show they are being consistent with their past: that they are indeed
the 'same old Tories'. Accordingly, a few pages later the manifesto
returns to the consistency of approach during Cameron's leadership:

> We know that this is an ambitious plan. A profoundly
> optimistic vision. It is also an authentically Conservative
> vision: sound money, backing enterprise, trusting people.
> The journey we embarked on four and a half years ago
> was all about applying this Conservative approach to the
> progressive challenges of our age: making opportunity
> more equal; fighting poverty and inequality; improving the
> environment and general well-being. So our creed today
> is progressive Conservatism; and this is an unashamedly
> progressive Conservative manifesto. (p ix)

So the Cameron Conservatives see what they are proposing as
demonstrating continuity with core Conservative principles. Yet, they
also make an explicit attempt to link these principles with a progressive
agenda, and see no contradiction in doing so. They are quite open
about their desire to appear progressive and to focus on issues which
traditionally have been more closely linked to the Labour party.

It is therefore significant that the manifesto states:'We believe there is such thing as society, it's just not the same thing as the state' (p vii). This, of course, is a direct reference to, and rebuttal of, a famous phrase of Mrs Thatcher's. Needless to say, Mrs Thatcher is not mentioned specifically here, but this can be seen as clear attempt to differentiate Cameron's brand of Conservatism from his illustrious and controversial predecessor. However, the second part of the phrase – 'it's just not the same as the state' – can also be seen as a tempering of any implied criticism of Thatcher, and might allow the 2010 version of the Conservatives to claim that they are not being hostile to Thatcher's intent, but only reinterpreting her statement for the current times. The phrase might be seen as an attempt to separate Cameron from Thatcher without it being too fundamental a break.

However, to be fair, this phrase does link to the main themes of the manifesto. The Conservatives argue that what is needed is 'fundamental change: from big government that presumes to know best, to the Big Society that trusts in the people for ideas and innovation' (p viii). This idea of trust is restated on the following page:'As Conservatives, we trust people. We believe that if people are given more responsibility, they will behave more responsibly' (p ix). The Conservatives are arguing that the Labour government has taken responsibility away from people, and sought to do things on their behalf rather than trusting them to get the key decisions right themselves.

The manifesto is based around three programmes for reform: building a new economic model, building the Big Society, and reforming the political system so that people have more power and control over their lives. A consistent theme across all three of these programmes is that the Labour government has failed and is leaving behind serious problems in need of a fundamental change of approach.

The biggest issue facing the country in 2010, by common consent, was the state of the public finances and how any new government would deal with this. Accordingly, the manifesto states early on (p 7) that urgent action is needed to reduce both public debt and the deficit. Yet this issue receives slightly less than three pages, and no detailed plans are spelt out. This, as we shall see, is the key difference between the pre-election manifesto and post-election coalition agreement. The deficit is mentioned, but the Conservatives seem to be determined to be optimistic and to focus on positive changes rather than austerity and any difficulties that will be caused by cutting government spending. Accordingly, much space is given over to considering the Big Society. Creating such a society involves a promise to 'redistribute power from the centre to individuals, families and local communities. We will give public sector workers back their professional autonomy' (p 35). They describe the Big Society as: 'a society with much higher levels of personal, professional, civic and corporate responsibility; a society where people come together to solve problems and improve life for themselves and their communities; a society where the leading force for progress is social responsibility, not state control' (p 37).

The Conservatives are seeking to create higher levels of citizen engagement and activism, where adults volunteer for community projects as a matter of course and where citizens have a direct say in how public services are managed and prioritised. But, the Conservatives were careful to state that this is not to be taken as a recipe for laissez-faire: 'building the big society is not just a question of the state stepping back and hoping for the best: it will require an active role for the state. The state must take action to agitate for, catalyse and galvanise social renewal. We must use the state to help remake society' (p 37). We might see this as another deliberate attempt to differentiate themselves from the Thatcherite legacy. They are not anti-state or libertarian in their approach.[4] Instead the manifesto makes an explicit reference to a core conservative, indeed Burkean, notion:

> Our reform agenda is designed to empower communities to come together to address local issues. For example, we will enable parents to start new schools, empower communities to take over local amenities such as parks and libraries that are under threat, give neighbourhoods greater control of the planning system, and enable residents to hold police to account in neighbourhood beat meetings. These policies will give new powers and rights to neighbourhood group, the 'little platoons' of civil society – and the institutional building blocks of the Big Society. (p 38)

This reference to the 'little platoons' is, of course, a direct reference to Burke and his idea of natural local allegiances that form the bedrock of any society (Burke, 1999b). As we have seen, for Burke society is made up of many different interests that coalesce around local issues and concerns.

In order to encourage the 'little platoons', the manifesto argues for a shift away from top-down control towards localism and decentralisation:

> We believe in people power – and today the information revolution gives us the practical tools to realise that philosophy. So we plan to change Britain with a sweeping

redistribution of power: from the state to citizens; from the government to Parliament; from Whitehall to communities; from Brussels to Britain; from bureaucracy to democracy. Taking power away from the political elite and handing it to the man and woman in the street. Using decentralisation, accountability and transparency, we will weaken the old political elites, give people power, fix our broken politics and restore people's faith that if we act together things can change. *This is a new agenda for a new politics.* (p 63, emphasis added)

Here is an explicit reference to the idea of a new politics, and with it some sense of what it might mean. It is one of decentralisation and an end to top-down politics. The Conservatives wish see an end to the creeping centralisation of political power and put forward changes to the planning system as well as reform to political institutions in order to achieve this. As we shall see with the agreement with the Liberal Democrats, the idea of decentralisation and devolving power becomes a core element of the new politics of the coalition. However, we should note, as we shall also see below, that the idea of restoring the people's faith in politics was also one identified by the Conservatives in 1979 and so is perhaps not especially representative of a new politics so much as a consistent claim made by opposition parties.

However, it was the idea of decentralisation that opened the Conservatives up to a degree of parody, in that it might be suggested that they were proposing something like do-it-yourself public services, where citizens would have to do things for themselves rather than relying on professionals. This, needless to say, was not quite what the Conservatives were envisaging. However, the problem, as we saw in Chapter Four, was that this idea had not really been floated much before the election campaign. The Conservatives had not prepared the ground for their Big Society rhetoric and had not developed a consistent narrative around it.

Indeed the Conservative's radicalism only went so far and they were keen to stress their commitment to the NHS, claiming that they now are 'the party of the NHS' (p 45) with a promise to back its current level of funding and to maintain it as a free service at the point of use. While they wished to reform the management of the NHS, they were also very anxious to be seen as supporting its core principles and its continued funding.

But there is a more general problem with the Big Society rhetoric that we should perhaps touch on here. The Conservatives wish to devolve power to communities and individuals, yet this is to be done by central government dictat. The creation of the Big Society is itself a top-down solution to the problems of Britain. It may be necessary, but there is still something of a paradox here. This connects with contemporary criticisms of the Thatcher and Major governments who too tried to reduce the influence of government but actually felt they had to use government to do this. Both Gamble (1988) and Jenkins (1995) showed that past Conservative governments had to strip power from local government and intermediate institutions in order to achieve their aims of liberating individual households and companies from the state. This meant, of course, that central government was also able to set the limits of decentralisation and so maintain control. It is too early to state whether the same will apply to Cameron's government, but the initial approach is the same: it is the government that is initiating decentralisation and on its terms.

In the manifesto there is an explicit attempt to link Conservatism to conservation and green issues. Indeed nearly 10% of the manifesto is taken up with this issue. The Conservatives suggest that they have a 'vision for a greener Britain' (p 89). This entails greater energy efficiency, care for the countryside and natural habitats. This, they argue, 'is a Conservative vision for our future, and it is based on Conservative values. We believe that it is our responsibility to create a clean and healthy environment to pass on to our children' (p 89). We might see an implicit link here with another of Burke's idea of society consisting not merely of those currently present, but also of the dead and the unborn (Burke, 1999b). Politics therefore becomes a matter of holding in trust what our ancestors have given us so that we can pass it on our children. Accordingly, a few pages later we find: 'Conservatives understand the inherent value of conserving things, and we know the importance of ensuring that we provide a good quality of life for future generations' (p 95).

The Conservatives, in seeking to achieve this vision, suggest that they 'will go with the grain of human nature, creating new incentives and market signals which reward people for doing the right thing' (p 89). As we shall see, the phrase 'the grain of human nature' is one that the Conservatives have also used in the past. It is suggestive of an emphasis on common sense rather than abstractions. The Conservatives seek not to reform human nature, or wish it were different than it is, but to work with it to create change.

The final section of the manifesto considers foreign affairs. This is interesting in that it explicitly discusses the idea of a liberal Conservatism:

A Conservative government's approach will be based on liberal Conservative principles. Liberal, because Britain must be open and engaged with the world, supporting human rights and championing the cause of democracy and the rule of law at every opportunity. But Conservative, because our policy must be hard-headed and practical, dealing with the world as it is and not as we wish it were. (p 109)

However, despite this link with liberal values, the Conservatives are, they say, 'sceptical about grand utopian schemes to remake the world' (p 109). They go on: 'We will work patiently with the grain of other societies, but will always support liberal values because they provide the foundations for stability and prosperity' (p 109). Again, while they speak of liberal values, unlike the Blair government they do not wish to impose a particular vision, but instead respect national cultures. This, we might suggest, is entirely typical of the Conservative approach: practical, pragmatic and accepting of the world as it is. It is also a tacit rejection of the neo-conservatism served up by the Bush administration in the USA.

Overall, we might suggest that the manifesto was not exactly a shallow document. It sought to present a distinctive vision, and it was certainly a more substantial document than that presented by the Conservatives to the electorate in 1979. The problem, however, was that the 2010 manifesto had to do the job of both outlining a new idea for government – the Big Society – and to present a reasonably detailed policy programme. It found itself trying to explain something new and distinctive a mere three weeks before an election. As we shall see, this was a not a mistake made by the Conservatives in 1979.

The manifesto was followed up by *A Contract Between the Conservative Party and You* (Conservative Party, 2010b) that was released on 4 May, just two days before the election. This was a brief summary of the manifesto, stressing the three themes of changing politics, changing the economy and changing society – the idea of change being quite explicit here – but dressed up as a contract. In particular, the contract stressed the idea of having to work together: 'We will only get our economy moving, mend our broken society and reform our rotten political system if we all get involved, take responsibility, and work together' (no page number).

As we considered in Chapter Four, the idea of the Big Society was somewhat underplayed in the latter stages of the election and the manifesto did not have the desired effect of creating a distinctive narrative. In order to become Prime Minister David Cameron had to form a coalition with the Liberal Democrats. Forming this coalition involved some compromises and policies dropped, particularly a softening of the rhetoric on Europe and a downplaying of explicit support for marriage and increasing inheritance tax thresholds. The programme for the coalition was outlined in a formal document entitled *The Coalition: Our Programme for Government* (Cabinet Office, 2010). There is much that is carried through from the Conservative manifesto, but the rhetoric of the coalition document is quite different.

The coalition's programme was based on three principles: freedom, fairness and responsibility. These can certainly be read across from the Conservative manifesto especially those of freedom and responsibility, although fairness too is mentioned. Fairness, however, was the key concept of the Liberal Democrat election campaign (Liberal Democrats, 2010). Subsequent to the election, and as the government has announced its spending and reform plans, the notion of fairness has become central to political debate.

Another clear link with the Conservatives' earlier documents is the 'conviction that the days of big government are over; that centralisation and top-down control have proved a failure' (p 7). But this too was something the Liberal Democrats stressed throughout the election campaign. What this shows is that there were ready areas of commonality between the two parties, sufficient to put forward a comprehensive programme for government.

The document contains a detailed list of policy priorities listed alphabetically, and so the relative importance of each policy is not readily apparent. However, we do not get too far into the alphabet before reading that 'the most urgent task facing this coalition is to tackle the record debts, because without sound finances, none of our ambitions will be deliverable' (p 7). This is a key difference with the pre-election material, with no longer any attempt to downplay the scale of the financial issues facing the government. The coalition agreement is quite explicit in its commitment to tackle the deficit and this creates a rather more downbeat effect compared with the sunny disposition of the manifesto. Indeed, at the very back of the document in large print, as if to overshadow everything that has gone before, the agreement states:

> The deficit reduction programme takes precedence over any of the other measures in this agreement, and the speed of implementation of any measures that have a cost to the public finances will depend on decisions to be made in the Comprehensive Spending Review. (p 35)

Prior to the Review, in June 2010, the government had an Emergency Budget (HM Treasury, 2010a) that outlined the government's approach to tackling the deficit. This made it all too clear that deficit reduction would not be shirked with the government planning to eradicate the deficit by the end of the Parliament in 2015 as opposed to the Brown government's plan merely to halve it in that time.

As we saw in Chapter Four, the Comprehensive Spending Review took place in October 2010 and laid out detailed plans for departmental spending for the duration of the Parliament. The Review makes it clear that fundamental reforms to welfare, as well as areas such as defence and higher education, form an intrinsic part of the government's planning. So the welfare budget is to be cut, but at the same time fundamental reforms are to be introduced to encourage work and end welfare dependency. Again, we can suggest this is an example of a pragmatic approach to government based on the need to react to circumstance. However, there has led to some reining in of the optimistic pre-election rhetoric in favour of financial realism.

But some of the change in approach since the election is clearly due to the influence of the Liberal Democrats. This is noticeable in some policy areas, particularly electoral reform where the Conservatives were forced to offer a referendum on the alternative vote system. But, there is also some moderation of language in terms of how government can affect change more generally. For example, gone is the language of government working with the 'grain of human nature' and using incentives and market signals. Instead the document states that the government, while still being against over-heavy bureaucracy, will find 'intelligent ways to encourage, support and enable people to make better choices for themselves' (p 8). One is left to speculate what this might mean, but clearly there has been some attempt here to deal with Liberal Democrat sensitivities about the role of markets. We might see this as connecting with the heightened focus on fairness as the main way in which the Liberal Democrats have altered the focus of the Conservatives. There is less of the traditional Conservative rhetoric and more of a stress on fairness and freedom. Accordingly, the document is strong on both civil liberties issues, such as the cancelling of identity cards and political reforms.

So where the two parties have common ground is on developing what they consider to be a progressive agenda. As we saw in Chapter Four, several commentators have pointed to the fact that Cameron might find working with the Liberal Democrats rather more congenial than dealing with the right of the Conservative party. While, of course, this is not admitted to in the coalition agreement, there is certainly an attempt to present the coalition's programme not simply as a collection of disparate elements from both parties' programmes. Instead they claim to have 'found that a combination of our parties' best ideas and attitudes has produced a programme for government that is more radical and comprehensive than our individual manifestos' (p 8). The coalition agreement stresses the radical and progressive nature of the new government, as if the Liberal Democrats have allowed Cameron to give free rein to his progressive instincts. Accordingly, the document states:

> We arrive at this programme for government a strong, progressive coalition inspired by the values of freedom, fairness and responsibility. This programme is for five years of partnership government driven by those values. We believe that it can deliver radical, reforming government, a stronger society, a smaller state, and power and responsibility in the hands of every citizen. Great change and real progress lie ahead. (p 8)

There are clear references here to key concepts in the Conservative manifesto, particularly the stress on responsibility and a smaller state, but there is no explicit reference to the Big Society, instead merely the need for a 'stronger' one.[5] We find a promise of 'great change and real progress'. This is not exactly different from the Conservative manifesto, but rather we might see it as an attempt to emphasise a particular thrust, as if the coalition with the Liberal Democrats liberates Cameron from the need to take all parts of his party along with him.

This does not mean that the coalition will be a success, and nor does it mean that it will actually achieve 'great change and real progress'. As we have seen, the overriding priority is dealing with the deficit, and this has meant difficult choices have had to be made, many of them less congenial to the Liberal Democrats than the Conservatives. However, what we can see is some consistency in Cameron running with a particular rhetoric, even as he has to bend this according to circumstance. This suggests that there might be something in the claim of a new politics just as it allows us to suggest that Cameron has shown a typically Conservative ability to react to circumstance. We need to see now whether this ability was shared by his illustrious predecessor in her attempt to unseat a Labour government.

What Thatcher said

As stated above, we have to be careful in comparing Cameron and Thatcher. The latter is no longer active in politics after a long, distinguished and controversial career. Mrs Thatcher is a politician who virtually everyone has an opinion of. Cameron, of course, is perhaps better known at the time of writing, but his career as Prime Minister is still very much in its infancy. The comparison that is made here, therefore, is restricted to what was said prior to Mrs Thatcher taking up office. Accordingly, I aim to deal with two documents in this section: one from 1976 outlining Conservative principles and the other the 1979 manifesto. As I have stated above, the documents are not exact correlates and this is because the two leaders took a different approach in preparing for their first election. We should therefore be cautious in what judgements we make. Having said this, however, there are some fascinating and instructive connections, as well as some important differences.

The 1976 document, entitled *The Right Approach* (Conservative Party, 1976) is interesting in that it lays out a particular rhetoric that became identifiable later as Thatcherism. But it also presents a particular set of priorities that is largely followed in the manifesto three years later. *The Right Approach* is a document of over 70 pages that seeks to present the principles of the Conservatives a year after the election of Margaret Thatcher as party leader. It is written in a totally different style to the 2010 documents. The 1979 document seeks to build a detailed case and to back this up with arguments, rather than merely making a series of assertions. Of course, the document was not meant as an election statement, but it did seek to present a specific vision in much the same way as the 2010 Conservatives intended with their manifesto.

The tone of the 1976 document is rather less optimistic than those of 2010. Indeed it suggests that the country is facing a crisis. There is considerable pessimism about the state of the country and considerable stress is placed on the failings of the Labour government led first by Harold Wilson and then James Callaghan. The Conservatives argued that the country was facing a point of no return and that the next election was something of a last chance. Were Labour to continue in office the country might not be able to recover:

> It is the task of the Conservative party today to restore hope and confidence to a disillusioned British people. Without the prospect of an alternative government with realistic policies, offending neither against common sense

nor against the instincts of the majority, the very survival
of parliamentary democracy could be threatened – by
the increasing alienation of the electors, if not in the
end by direct action from exasperated pressure groups.
(Conservative Party, 1976, p 7)

So there is real sense of an imperative for change running through *The
Right Approach* as it outlines the aims and intentions of the Conservatives
building up to the next election. The impression one gets from reading
this document beside the 2010 manifesto is that the problems must
have been much more severe in 1976, even though we know this not
to be the case. Unlike 2010, there is no attempt here to downplay
the seriousness of the situation the Conservatives felt was facing the
country. Indeed, if anything, the opposite is the case.

The document begins with an attempt to put the state of Britain
and its economy in 1976 into context. There is a discussion of the
international situation over the previous few years, dealing with the
failing economy and the recent oil crisis. In setting up the issues the
document quotes Alexis de Tocqueville at length and seeks to create a
deliberate link with the conservative intellectual tradition. Indeed, the
whole document shows a striking intellectual confidence and a sense of
certainty that would prove typical of the Conservatives under Thatcher.

But, like the 2010 manifesto, *The Right Approach* is still very much
a product of its time, and sets up its argument in relation to the issues
facing Britain in 1976. It is extremely critical of the class-based politics
it took to be at the heart of Labour's approach and felt the need to
make explicit its opposition to socialism of both the Marxist and social
democratic varieties. It is this debate against an apparently real and
active socialism (and with the Soviet Union still a major world power,
this was an international as well as a national concern) that is striking
and shows the distance that politics has travelled since the 1970s. This
is also seen in the issues that the document focused on, with detailed
discussions on industrial relations, the trade unions and on housing.
These were not issues that featured very strongly in the 2010 election
despite an ongoing series of strikes by British Airways cabin crew and
a major housing market crash only two years before the election.

One way in which *The Right Approach* goes beyond the 2010
documents is in the claims it makes for Conservatism. Cameron's
manifesto states that his new approach is consistent with Conservative
values. However, the 1976 document not only states what Conservatism
is, but why it is a superior ideology for dealing with the problems of

a complex society such as Britain. The first necessary element, they argue, is pragmatism and a willingness to listen:

> Those who govern must be more ready both to listen and to examine the facts of life objectively. We believe that in both these respects Conservatives have the advantage of their Labour opponents, since we are not blinkered by a Socialist ideology that assumes the omni-competence of the State and is rooted in a theory of ownership and class conflict already decades out of date. (p 7)

Labour, they suggest, was beholden to a particular dogma, which meant that it did not believe it had to listen to the people. They already had the answers, pre-supplied by their socialist ideals. The Conservatives argued that, by way of contrast, they were pragmatic and prepared to listen and then base their form of governance on what they took to be the interests of the people. But we should also note the comment that they saw socialism as outdated. The Conservatives here portrayed the Labour party as living in the past, holding on to a redundant ideology. Instead it is the Conservatives who were the party of the present and the future. There was no explicit mention of progress here, but the implication was clear.

They described their approach as a philosophy of balance, which 'matches the manners, the customs, the laws, the traditions of the British people' (p16). However, they did not leave their argument there, but rather they enunciated their philosophy in some detail, and in a manner that would be unthinkable in a political document in 2010:

> Man is both an individual and a social being, and all political philosophies have sought to accommodate these two, often conflicting, elements in human nature. Conservatism has always represented a balance between the two, arguing against Liberal individualists for man's social role and against Socialists for the right of the individual to develop as far and as fast as he can, choosing freely from a wide range of opportunities while recognising his duties towards his fellows.
>
> We have laid particular stress on the individual and his freedom in recent years because Socialism has tipped the balance so far the other way. Moreover, many of the developments of modern industrial society have tended

to dehumanise life and threaten the individuality and independence of men and women.

But we do not base our approach solely on the individual, on the view that the only role of society is to provide a framework of laws within which individual opportunities can flourish without becoming self-destructive. If we were to do this, a number of other things in which Conservatives believe – patriotism, loyalty, duty – would be meaningless. Man *is* an individual, answerable to himself. But he is also a citizen, the member of a complex network of small communities which go to make up society – family, neighbourhood, church, voluntary organisation, work-place and so on. (Conservative Party, 1976, pp 16–17, original emphasis)

We can see this as a rather more complex statement of the Conservative view of civil society summarised by the one-liner in the 2010 document that 'there is such a thing as society, it's just not the same thing as the state' (Conservative Party, 2010a, p vii). We can see the idea of Burke's 'little platoons' implicit in the final sentence quoted above, where the individual is also taken to be 'a citizen, the member of a complex network of small communities': this is indeed precisely what Burke's idea consisted of (Burke, 1999b). So the Conservatives both in 1976 and in 2010 referred to a form of Burkean conservatism that recognised and encouraged the basic building blocks of civic society. And just like the 2010 manifesto, *The Right Approach* was clear that the state had a role:

> Enterprise comes first from individuals, not from 'National Boards'. But this does not make us a *laissez-faire* party. We have always conceded that the State should have a role as the trustee of the whole community in any economic system, holding the balance between different interests. (p 18)

It is individuals who create the wealth of a society, but the state has a role to ensure that no one interest overrides all others. This sense of the state as trustee is perhaps a less activist approach to that taken by the Conservatives in 2010 who saw the role of the state as catalysing and galvanising individuals into action. However, it is still clear that both generations of Conservatives were not advocating the minimal state.

This though did not mean an emphasis on intervention. The role of the government should remain a limited one and accordingly the Conservatives stated that they would:

> promise less in opposition, to practise restraint in government and to give choice and freedom back to the people, will help to reduce the burden of government and to restore the faith of the public in those they elect. We must also increase the authority of Parliament and its power over the Executive. (p 43)

It seems, then, that the year 2010 was not unique for experiencing both disillusionment on the part of the electorate and a commitment to reform and clean up politics by politicians. The quote above could quite easily have slotted into the 2010 manifesto of the Conservatives, and indeed any of the other major parties, and not have looked out of place.

A further similarity is that both generations claim that Conservatism is rooted in common sense, in the natural taken-for-granted responses of ordinary individuals. The 1976 Conservatives link this to their philosophy of balance when they state that:

> The balance which we seek has its roots not only in a distinctive, if too rarely articulated, Conservative approach, but also in basic common sense. That has always been one of the great strengths of Conservatism. The facts of life invariably *do* turn out to be Tory. (p 19, original emphasis)

The last sentence here is a wonderful example of the intellectual confidence of the Conservative in 1976. They made a clear link between the common sense of individuals and Conservatism and so suggested that there was something quite natural about being a Tory. Conservatism is rooted in the concrete actions of individuals and therefore it is the role of government to ensure that individual action is supported:

> Conservatives believe that it is people that matter, not sterile dogmas and 'social engineering'. We believe that the individual citizen should have more encouragement to provide for his own future, that it should always pay to work, that a sound family life lies at the heart of a healthy society, and that the welfare of the community depends upon the strong helping the weak. (p 57)

The document concluded with a concise statement of what the Conservatives stood for in 1976 and what would form the basis of their pitch to the electorate:

> Our policies are designed to restore and defend individual freedom and responsibility. We mean to protect the individual from excessive interference by the State or by organisations licensed by the State, to stop the drift of power away from the people and their democratic institutions, and to give them more power as citizens, as owners and as consumers. We shall do this by better financial management, by reducing the proportion of the nation's wealth consumed by the State, by steadily easing the burden of Britain's debts, by lowering taxes when we can, by encouraging home ownership, by taking the first steps towards making this country a nation of worker owners, by giving parents a greater say in the better education of their children.
>
> Conservatives do not believe that they have a monopoly of the truth. But we do believe that the approach we outline today is the right one for this country, in tune with the instincts and views of the overwhelming majority of our fellow-citizens. There has seldom been a time when our party has had a greater opportunity to recruit the intellectual and political support of the nation. There has never been a time when the nation needed the Conservative Party more. (p 71)

This, therefore, was a substantial statement of the Conservative position, which provided some specific policy commitments, such as trade union laws and the Right to Buy, but which embedded these policies into a principled argument. It provided a justification for Conservatism that was not just based on assertions, but committed itself to argument and critique. It was a more serious and austere document than those published in 2010, even as it lacked the latter's presentation and accessibility.

The 1979 election manifesto (Conservative Party, 1979) can be seen as a pared down version of *The Right Approach*, being only 40% as long (and less than 30% the length of the 2010 manifesto). Its structure is largely the same as the document of three years earlier, as are much of the contents, including the commitments to limit the actions of trade unions and to allow council tenants to buy their dwellings. Like in 1976, the Conservatives argued that the stakes for the country were really very high: 'This election may be the last chance we have to reverse that process, to restore the balance of power in favour of the people. It is therefore the most crucial election since the war' (Conservative Party, 1979, no page number). The Conservatives wished to convey a sense of urgency; that the country needed to act decisively to deal with its many longstanding problems.

However, the tone was not unduly pessimistic, rather one of a cautious and realistic optimism:

> Our country's relative decline is not inevitable. We in the Conservative Party think we can reverse it, *not* because we think we have all the answers but because we think we have the one answer that matters most. We want to work *with the grain* of human nature, helping people to help themselves – and others. This is the way to restore that self-reliance and self-confidence which are the basis of personal responsibility and national success. (no page number)

The Conservatives again claimed that they were working with how people actually are and basing their approach on common sense rather than dogma. Accordingly, they ended the manifesto with a clarion call based on an assertion of this common-sense realism:

> Most people, in their hearts, know that Britain has to come to terms with reality. They no longer have any time for politicians who try to gloss over the harsh facts of life. Most people want to be told the truth, and to be given a clear lead towards the action needed for recovery.
>
> The years of make-believe and false optimism are over. It is time for a new beginning. (no page number)

New politics, or what?

All political parties, of whatever generation, like to make unqualified claims about their own aims and achievements. As we have seen, the Conservatives, of both the Thatcher and Cameron vintage, have argued that they wish to remake politics and deal with crises not of their own making. Both suggest that they represent a considerable change with what went before. Our purpose here is not to comment on whether they did, or are likely to, achieve their aims. Rather we are concerned with what they said and what this shows.

Clearly, we can point to several similarities in addition to the declaration of themselves as representing real change. Both the 1976 and 2010 generations argued that they were going with the grain of human nature. They suggested that they understood human nature and what motivates and incentivises people. This, according to the Conservatives, is not because of any particular ideology or dogma but because of a preparedness to listen and to pay a close attention to the answers.

This is quite important in that it suggests a particular attitude towards change. The Conservatives in the 1970s and 2010 called for change, but they did this without articulating an overarching vision. Other than stating that they wished individuals to be freer and more responsible, they did not offer a particular picture of what they wished to remake society into. Their views were not utopian, but based on an understanding of what was wrong with society as it now stands. Neither set of Conservatives was seeking to thoroughly transform society in any structural sense, merely to undo many of the faults of their predecessors. Accordingly, we read frequent references to common sense and realism. They wished to ensure that existing and long established institutions work better.

We have also seen that the Conservatives in 1976 and 2010 sought to restore faith in politics. They wished to remove the taint of the recent past and return to a vision of politics as it once was. While, following the 2009 parliamentary expenses scandal, Cameron's Conservatives had no alternative but to refer to this need to remake politics, this was by no means a new issue.

A further point of commonality is the link between the individual and the community, be it described as the citizen and the community as in 1976, or the Big Society and the 'little platoons' in 2010. This Burkean sense of the unbreakable link between individual and society – that we are both private individuals and social beings – is an enduring feature of conservatism. We might say that this idea of the indivisibility of the individual from the social is what gives conservatism its purpose and differentiates it from other ideologies.

The links between Thatcher and Cameron are not just based on content but also on approach, and these are perhaps more important in telling us something about the nature of Conservatism. While the tenor of the documents is certainly different, and they are certainly distinct stylistically, all the documents show a high level of pragmatism and the ability to shift according to circumstance. There is an expedience in the approach shown by the Conservatives. This is obviously most noticeable in the 2010 documents, which chart the shift from a wholly Conservative approach to one of coalition. But the documents of the

Thatcher period also show a perspective that is essentially reactive. The essence of Conservatism is the reaction to circumstance and these documents provide ample evidence of this.

Second, we can note that all these documents, and despite the rather demotic style of the 2010 manifesto, show a marked lack of abstraction. They are concerned with the world as it is and are not based on some abstract or utopian principle. The Conservatives accept the world, and the people within it, as they currently are and not as they ought to be. As we have seen, conservatives are concerned with the surface of things and this is clearly manifest in the documents we have been looking at.

So what can we conclude from this about the newness or otherwise of Cameron's Conservatism? I have asked already whether it is really contradictory to argue that Cameron represents both a new politics and 'the same old Tories', and I want to suggest that it is indeed possible to be both old and new. Politics, in a very important sense, is always 'new'. The circumstances in which a political party finds itself are always unique and distinct. Issues have to be faced which are unpredictable; situations occur which have no precedent; politicians have to act with only partial knowledge, and sometimes when they are not even aware of what it is that they do not know. So, if we accept that politics is always based on circumstance, then it must always, in a sense, be 'new'. It is not based entirely on what has gone before, but on what arises and what it is possible to do to deal with this issue. This, we might think, reduces the very idea of a 'new politics' to something of a banality. However, we need to factor in the incentives that politicians have to call attention to the newness of their situation and their means for dealing with it.

Newness, so to speak, works because democratic politics depends on it: it is this that creates the difference between parties and politicians and provides the electorate with some purpose in voting. We might even go so far as to suggest that a declaration of 'newness' shows that politics is actually always the same.

But there is a more substantial argument for linking newness to sameness. If we think about it for a moment would we actually want David Cameron, or indeed any politician, to act in a manner that was not predicated in some way on the past? Would we really want him to behave in such an unpredictable manner, so that we would have no idea what he was about to do and why? Do we not actually want, and expect, politicians to behave in a manner that is principled and therefore predictable? Politicians and political parties are expected to behave consistently and for a reason. If they did not, could we find it in ourselves to vote for them? Political parties start from certain principles and these determine how they respond to circumstance. So we would expect Cameron, just like any other Tory, to behave like the 'same old Tories'. For him to do anything else would be unprincipled and counterproductive.

This argument – that a politician is being entirely consistent with past principles through extolling newness – only seems strange or perverse if one does not appreciate the nature of conservatism as a broad and general ideological disposition. Once we accept that conservatism is about reacting we can appreciate just why Cameron has taken the steps that he has. So we should then see Cameron and the party he now leads as the same old Tories. But this is not to deride or insult them, whatever their political opponents may claim. It is instead to see them as proper conservatives, who take risks to protect that which they consider irreplaceable.

Notes

[1] Indeed a developing issue in 2010 was the number of public servants who were paid more than the Prime Minister and whether this could be justified. The level that the PM was paid was therefore seen as particularly important.

[2] The fact that the Labour party was led by a privileged former public school boy for 13 years undoubtedly helped.

[3] Of course, in this sense they were no different from Blair's Cabinet in 1997.

[4] However, as we shall see in the next section, the Conservatives had made a similar point in 1976.

[5] Having said this, the government, and the Prime Minister in particular, have not backed off from the Big Society agenda and it has formed a central part in the government's thinking particularly with regard to localism and decentralisation.

SIX

The same new Tories

Introduction

Conservatism is both simple, in the manner that it eschews theory, but also complex because it seeks to refrain from prediction. It relies on a call to common sense and basic human nature, on an appreciation of incentives and the manner in which people respond to protect and further their individual and collective interests. Yet conservatives only react to circumstance; and of course, we can never react in advance. Therefore, we can never properly state what the future might hold and nor can we seek to pre-empt it.

The flexibility and adaptability of conservatism, and the Conservative party, over the centuries are due to this reactive nature. But this can also create some confusion regarding just what conservatism is and where its interests lie. Conservatives will describe themselves differently in different places and at different times. They will seek alliances with others, which at other times might be seen as unlikely or even perverse. Yet they still remain conservative.

We have seen that conservatism is an attempt to preserve what is valuable. But we have also seen that the British Conservative party, the inheritors of the great tradition leading away from Edmund Burke, now consider themselves to be both liberal and progressive. David Cameron has sought to distance his party and himself from more traditional right-wing ideas, much to the disgruntlement of some media commentators and party members. Most offensive of all has been the forming of a coalition with an apparently left of centre party and then claiming to represent a new politics that leaves behind narrow party interest.

However, the Conservative–Liberal Democrat government led by Cameron is the only form of Conservative government on offer: the die-hards might not much like what they got in May 2010, but the alternative was more of the Labour party. We might be able to imagine a more pure or authentic form of Conservatism, but we are not going to get it, at least not unless many things change. In the meantime we might as well get used to what we actually do have and seek to understand it more fully.

That has been the purpose of this book and, in this last chapter, I wish to come to something of a conclusion about the nature of Conservatism and what to make of Cameron's new politics. I have, I hope, already made it clear what my view is: I have already stated that Cameron does represent a new politics, but that this is what we would expect from the 'same old Tories'. Conservatism has a history of reinvention, but can do this by and large without renouncing key elements of the conservative tradition. What remains, therefore, is simply to make this explicit and to consider some of the implications that I believe flow from this conclusion.

A balanced approach

Conservatism is not an extreme doctrine: it does not seek to transgress established patterns. Instead it aims to take a balanced approach to government. We have considered this approach throughout this book, alighting particularly on the ideas of Edmund Burke (1999a, 1999b, 1999c, 1999d). Burke suggested that politics existed on a nice equipoise. It is in a delicate balance and on either side of it are dangerous precipices. Politics is settled within a dangerous environment and it is all too possible to slip down into the pit and be lost. And once we have tilted too far so that we fall, we cannot pull ourselves back out. Regaining our balance after a fall is near impossible and accordingly we should take steps to ensure that we do not tilt too far in the first place. We should therefore not make any sudden or unexpected moves that might tip the balance. Instead we should only seek actions that stabilise and maintain a degree of harmony.

Burke's ideal is government by increments. It is governing that rejects the large leap and the sudden change of direction. There is too much risk involved. To change the metaphor, we have discussed the tightrope view of politics on several occasions. This is a similar idea. Government, we might suggest, is like stepping out onto a tightrope that straddles two sides of a deep canyon. We can only get from one side to the other with extreme care, through concentration and perhaps a degree of luck. But we also need a high level of expertise and a steely nerve, and these are qualities that might be quite rare. Not many would dare to attempt to walk the tightrope and perhaps even fewer would actually be able to.

Oakeshott (1962) also sees government in these terms: it is a difficult and dangerous activity that is best left to those with the requisite skill and courage. This is because the stakes are very high, the costs of failure so great and the possibility of error so large. As we stand on one side of the cliff we can see that there is only one way across – the tightrope

– and it will be an extremely difficult and hazardous crossing. It is something, we might think, that is best left to someone else who has had the training, who has done it before and so has shown they have the steely nerve and temperament for the task.

But there is a further point made by Oakeshott. In reality, there is no purpose to tightrope walking other than the activity itself. Indeed, Oakeshott reminds us that there are indeed many such activities that are ends in themselves, like fishing or friendship. There is no end here other than the activity itself. Oakeshott argues that politics is of a similar nature: governing is an end in itself and it has no other purpose than its own maintenance. For Oakeshott, and also for Burke, governing has sufficient justification in itself not to need any other purpose. Societies, as Scruton (2001) reminds us, are made up of individuals and institutions, all with their own ends and interests, which can only be expressed in the present. The life that they are leading is all that they have. These individuals and institutions do not exist for some other purpose beyond themselves and so they cannot legitimately be used in a manner that makes them subservient to any other purpose. It is not the role of government to use those currently living to meet some future purpose. Government exists to maintain the present and only through doing this can it ensure that there will be a future where individuals and institutions still have ends that they can seek to meet.

However, it is also true that we could not expect any modern government to state its case in these terms. To suggest that it sought to govern merely for the sake of governing would doubtless be seen as cynical and unprincipled. It would imply that politicians only want office for its own sake and to exercise power without expressing any purpose or vision. A modern government must claim to have a purpose and a coherent plan that it has presented before the electorate. It has made its pitch and sufficiently inspired the voters to be given a chance to govern.

It is perhaps difficult to imagine a totally passive and pragmatic government. Who would vote for a political party that had no programme other than a promise that it would react to events? Could we trust a party that claimed no purpose other than to stay in office? This party would fail to inspire us and so lack the means to get into power.

Yet all politicians and governments claim that they are responsive and pragmatic. They claim that they eschew ideology and do not have a preconceived view of the world. Modern democratic politicians see no virtue in overt ideology, claiming to take decisions based on evidence, on the facts in front of them and without any preconceptions. They see excessive ideology as a criticism reserved for their opponents. However, politicians still argue that they will change things and that they have a purpose. They may not be ideological, but they are principled and they act for a reason. Political leaders seek to make grand speeches to inspire the population to act or to support their programme.

What this suggests is that we have to separate out the rhetoric, which is often unqualified and definitive, from the actual preparedness to act, which may be considerably more measured. As we saw in Chapter Five when discussing their 2010 manifesto, the Conservatives claimed to be progressive and radical, but it did not espouse a particular vision of deep-rooted social transformation. It wished to preserve many of institutions of modern Britain and simply make them work better.

In truth most government action is piecemeal, incremental and partial. Government tends to focus on what is possible, what is achievable, and this means taking things in stages. It is not possible to start with a 'year zero' approach, but to work with and through our existing institutions and forms of government, and we would not really want politics to be other than this. Governments do and should respond to circumstance rather than stick to a preconceived plan regardless of the circumstances.

So we can suggest that the rhetoric of politics might be distinct from the reality. The former governor of New York, Mario Cuomo, is reputed to have said that 'we campaign in poetry, but we govern in prose'. Politicians seek to inspire voters to lend them their support. But once in government, and faced with the reality of the daily grind of administration, they find the business a rather more prosaic one. Many of the things that they are faced with do not lend themselves to easy solutions, and many events arise which could not have been foreseen and therefore planned for. A government may not be able to reach a complete and final solution to any problem, but rather has to compromise to achieve the best that is possible in the conditions that pertain at the time.

This means that politics is circumstantial and politicians have no choice but to respond to this. Perhaps the most obvious differences in circumstance are between government and opposition and between campaigning for and holding office. Hence we might expect that political parties promise much, using their finest poetry, only to revert to prosaic compromises when in office. Adams (2007), in his biography of A.J. Balfour, presents several examples, from Irish Home Rule to Imperial Preference, where Balfour felt he had no choice but to compromise and go against his core beliefs. This was not, Adams argues, out of cynicism or because of any lack of resolve, but from a realisation that there was no real alternative within the accepted confines of the

British Constitution and the established political culture. By 1922 the alternative to Irish Home Rule and independence was civil war and bloodshed. Accordingly, Balfour saw that some sort of concession was unavoidable. He, therefore, accepted Irish independence, even though he had spent much of his political career defending the Union between Britain and Ireland. It would have been better, from Balfour's point of view, not to have found himself in this position, but once there the choices were limited.

We can say the same for Cameron: once, on 7 May 2010 and faced with the election result leaving him short of a majority, he had several possibilities routes of action as party leader. These involved trying to form a minority government or seeking a coalition with a willing ally. What was not either a realistic or a sensible option was sitting back and holding a post mortem on the outcome of the election. That could come later once a government was in place, and perhaps be better conducted by others with the leisure to do so. For the leader of the largest party, 19 seats short of a majority, Cameron had to act in a manner that would maximise his party's interest. This meant dropping some of his manifesto pledges on issues such as Inheritance Tax and support for marriage, and changing some of his rhetoric to match that of the Liberal Democrats. However, the purpose of the Conservative party is to govern and this was the only means on offer of achieving that. Cameron ensured that as much of his programme could be retained as possible based on the circumstances in which he found himself. He may have wished for something else, but he had no choice.

We should note here that the Conservatives were not the only ones who actively sought a compromise. The Liberal Democrats too gave up some their policies and joined with a party committed to retaining the nuclear deterrent and top-up fees for students at university. The Liberal Democrats as a result have faced a backlash from some of their voters who are angry that they have joined in with the Conservatives and there is indeed some unease about the programme of public spending cuts needed to cut the deficit. However, if the purpose of a political party is to gain power to implement some, if not all, of its policies then what else could we expect from the Liberal Democrat leadership, and is it really unprincipled for them to have acted as they did?

Similarly, the Labour party sought to form a coalition and were prepared to offer the Liberal Democrats a deal on proportional representation even though they had made no attempt to change the voting system themselves during their 13 years in office, despite a manifesto commitment in 1997 that they would do so. Electoral reform did not apparently suit them when they had large majorities and could rule on their own, but became enticing once they were threatened with opposition. So all the three main parties were prepared to compromise to achieve or retain power, and again we have to ask, why should they not have sought to do so? What other option have they in the complex political milieu in which they operate? From each of the parties' perspective, not compromising would be worse.

Enough politics

Conservatives appreciate that politics is not an all-consuming passion for most of the electorate. Depending on the issues and the circumstances, a majority of people will vote and show an interest in an election campaign. But once it is over they will get on with their lives and not concern themselves with the minutiae of post-election analysis. What matters is the result, not all of the workings-out. Most people are quite happy that there are politicians to take complex and important decisions for them. Of course, they will only support those they trust to do the right sort of things. But once they are assured of this they feel they can then return to their own interests.

This attitude was shown on the very evening that David Cameron became Prime Minister on 11 May 2010. The BBC followed the events of the evening on its main channel, BBC1, as Gordon Brown offered his resignation to the Queen and Cameron was asked to form a government. As a result several prime time programmes were cancelled or postponed including the long-running soap opera *Eastenders*. The result was that over a thousand people complained to the BBC about the rescheduling (Lee, 2010). What mattered to these people, and there were doubtless many more that felt indignant without making a formal complaint, was not the sense of history being made before their eyes, but rather of the annoyance that their regular entertainment for the night had been postponed.

However, should we actually see this as such a bad thing? We expect there to be a government and so 'they' – the political classes – should just get on with it and leave us alone. After all, on the following day, 12 May, the sun came up as normal, the schools and shops opened, the buses and trains ran and bills still came due. So what was there to fuss over?

We might see this as apathy, or as an uncaring attitude towards the big issues of the day, and there may indeed be something of this in this reaction to yet another 'Election Special'. However, we might equally see this reaction as a case of complacency, of a sense that things still work as they should and that we can depend on them. We feel we can rely on the usual structures and systems and we are heartily glad that there are others who are prepared to run them on our behalf. We might not trust them as much as we, or they, would like, and perhaps even fear that they might be taking advantage of the system for their own benefit: the MPs expenses scandal in 2009 provided us with ample ammunition for our scepticism. But what is the reason that we have politicians, if we cannot get on with our own lives and enjoy some peace and quiet? We are delighted to let those with the time and talents deal with politics and instead we will worry about cutting the grass and which school to send our children to.

Some might find this complacency regrettable and wish that more people were active in politics. But this attitude is not in any way unnatural: it is rather precisely how we would expect people in a healthy and functioning democracy to act. If things work well then there is no need to continually articulate our concerns: having voted, we can let others get on with the politics.

This, we might suggest, is the other side of the circumstantial or tightrope view of politics. The electorate are not ideological, but rather respond to issues and events. This, after all, is how government changes and parties gain support and fall from favour. When the electorate have had enough of one party they turn to another, and all that the politicians can do is to react to this. Only then can they expect to be given the reins of power. The electorate can now get back to their own lives and leave the politicians to concentrate on the difficult job of governing. Governing is necessary precisely to allow the rest of us to get on with what we consider to be important. Accordingly, we want competence, consistency and reliability and then to be left alone. We need to trust our politicians, but only so we can safely ignore them and get on with the important things.

There are no absolutes in politics

Conservatism, as I have described it here, is not a doctrine of absolutes. It does not deal in either/ors, friend versus enemy, or indeed any other simple dichotomy. This applies also to the division between progress and reaction. While it might be convenient to see politics in these terms it clearly misunderstands the nature of conservatism.

As we have seen, conservatism is a disposition. It is an attitude or an inclination, such that we would tend towards certain things and away from others. However, this inclination need not, and perhaps should not, be complete. Nor should it ever be unconditional and unqualified. Conservatives will have certain tendencies towards particular ideas, forms of government and social relations, but their allegiance to these might not be total, and there may indeed be some contradiction in the mix of ideas, forms and relations.

Politics, for the conservative, is a question of nuance and extent; it is often a concern for fine gradations of judgement about how far to go and when to stop. Much of this caution is due to the immediacy of events and the need to respond quickly. Often one issue might be so dominant that it crowds out all others, as is the case with the need to reduce the public deficit in 2010 or coming to terms with the terrorist attacks on New York and Washington on 11 September 2001. But even though these issues dominate the public consciousness and the work of politicians, there are still many other issues – what we might call the basic administration of government – which persist and need to be dealt with. Amid the 'high politics' of world events and crises there is still the need for day-to-day administration. This administration is continuous, repetitive and purposefully dull as it proceeds unnoticed behind the headlines of politics. Administrative change is often slow and piecemeal, and this is just as it should be: the engine can only be repaired and even re-modelled while it is still running. Administration still has functions to perform as it is being reformed.

This is to see government as a finely balanced machine, which can only be tinkered with. Political parties may express a vision for how they wish to govern, and this might help them to gain sufficient electoral support. However, this provides only a guide and has to be applied over an already existing pattern of operation and behaviour. Politicians are seldom able to choose where they start from and are never quite sure where they are being led. The art of this, however, is to give the impression that they are precisely where they wish to be and this is entirely down to their own preconceived plan.

An understanding of the lack of absolutes helps us to appreciate further the circumstantial nature of politics. The conservative will ask: 'How should I approach this specific problem?' They find themselves in a particular situation and have to respond. There will be a number of options they could take, and none of these might offer the desired certainty of outcome. But any action is only necessary because a particular problem exists and needs a response. Without the problem the conservative sees no need to act. A conservative has no preconceived doctrine with which to deal with any issue, but rather they have a disposition that allows them to approach a problem as a unique event rather than as something that must fit within a particular typology.

So we can see the general essence of the conservative approach is expedience. It is about recognising what is achievable and necessary, rather than ideal, and then reacting accordingly. Governing is therefore a process of adaptation rather than of first principles. The problem for the Conservative party between 1992 and 2005 was that they were in grave danger of forgetting the virtue of expedience and placed preconceived ideals above governing.

Of course, having the right model is no guarantee of success. The Conservatives did not achieve complete, or even some would suggest sufficient, success in 2010. Like Salisbury (Roberts, 1999) and Balfour (Adams, 2007) before him, Cameron could only govern through a coalition. But if this is all that it possible then all one can do is make the best of it. To those more ideologically motivated this might appear to be both reprehensible and unprincipled. Yet the alternative is impotence and the limited joys of opposition, something that had become all too familiar to the Conservative party.

Same new Tories

So to conclude, my argument can be simply stated, despite the considerable complexity of its effect: politics is always new. Politics is based on circumstance and, for the Conservative, it can be no other. Accordingly, this means that politics is always the same, in that it involves reacting to events. And again, how can it be any other?

So, of course, the Conservatives in 2010 are the same old Tories, and the new politics of the coalition with the Liberal Democrats merely proves this. This is not unprincipled, but the only means in which Conservative principles could be enacted within the conditions pertaining at the times. The alternative might well have been a situation where the institutions that the Conservatives hold dear would have been only further eroded by those who have a different view of the past, the present and the future.

This means that Cameron is no different from other Conservatives in being put in a unique position with only the conservative disposition at his disposal. And who knows how new and different the same old Tories will be in the future?

References

Adams, R. J.Q. (2007) *Balfour: The last grandee*, London: John Murray.

Appleby, J. (2010) *The relentless revolution: A history of capitalism*, New York: Norton.

Bale, T. (2010) *The Conservative party: From Thatcher to Cameron*, Cambridge: Polity Press.

Berlin, I. (1969) *Four essays on liberty*, Oxford: Oxford University Press.

Berlin, I. (1990) *The crooked timber of humanity*, London: Fontana.

Blair, T. (2010) *A journey*, London: Hutchinson.

Blond, P. (2010) *Red Tory: How Left and Right have broken Britain and how we can fix it*, London: Faber and Faber.

Boddy, M. (1992) 'From mutual interests to market forces', in C. Grant (ed) *Built to last? Reflections on British housing policy*, London: Roof, pp 40–9.

BBC (2010) General Election 2010 Results. (http://news.bbc.co.uk/1/shared/election2010/results/)

Burke, E. (1992) *Further reflections on the Revolution in France*, Indianapolis: Liberty Fund.

Burke, E. (1999a) *Select works of Edmund Burke, Volume 1*, Indianapolis: Liberty Fund.

Burke, E. (1999b) *Select works of Edmund Burke, Volume 2*, Indianapolis: Liberty Fund.

Burke, E. (1999c) *Select works of Edmund Burke, Volume 3*, Indianapolis: Liberty Fund.

Burke, E. (1999d) *Select works of Edmund Burke, miscellaneous writings*, Indianapolis: Liberty Fund.

Cabinet Office (2010) *The coalition: Our programme for government*, London: Cabinet Office.

CSJ (Centre for Social Justice) (2007) *Breakthrough Britain: Ending the costs of social breakdown*, London: Centre for Social Justice.

CSJ (Centre for Social Justice) (2009) *Dynamic benefits: Towards welfare that works*, London: Centre for Social Justice.

Conservative Party (1976) *The right approach*, London: Conservative Party (http://www.margaretthatcher.org/archive/displaydocument.asp?docid=109439).

Conservative Party (1979) *Conservative general election manifesto 1979*, London: Conservative Party (http://www.margaretthatcher.org/archive/displaydocument.asp?docid=110858).

Conservative Party (2010a) *Invitation to join the government of Britain: The Conservative manifesto 2010*, London: Conservative Party.

Conservative Party (2010b) *A contract between the Conservative party and you*, London: Conservative party (http://www.conservativeparty.com/Policy/Contract.aspx).

Curtice, J. (2010) 'The last post', *Parliamentary briefing* (http://www.parliamentarybrief.com/2010/05/the-last-post).

Devigne, R. (1994) *Recasting Conservatism: Oakeshott, Strauss, and the response to postmodernism*, New Haven, CT: Yale University Press.

Dooley, M. (2009) *Roger Scruton: The philosopher on Dover Beach*, London: Continuum.

Dutton, D. (2004) *A history of the Liberal Party*, Basingstoke: Palgrave Macmillan.

DWP (Department for Work and Pensions) (2010) *21st century welfare*, London: DWP.

Etzioni, A. (1993) *The spirit of community: Rights, responsibilities and the communitarian agenda*, London: Fontana.

Gamble, A. (1988) *The free economy and the strong state: The politics of Thatcherism*, Basingstoke: Macmillan.

Giddens, A. (1994) *Beyond Left and Right: The future of radical politics*, Cambridge: Polity.

Glover, S. (2010) 'Cameron didn't win because he was scared of sounding too Tory', *Daily Mail* (http://www.dailymail.co.uk/debate/article-1274946/UK-ELECTION-RESULTS-2010-Cameron-didnt-win-scared-sounding-Tory.html).

Gottfried, P. (2007) *Conservatism in America: Making sense of the American Right*, New York: Palgrave Macmillan.

Gray, J. (1993) *Beyond Left and Right: Markets, government and the common environment*, London: Routledge.

Gray, J. (2009) *Gray's anatomy: Selected writings*, London: Allen Lane.

Green, E. (2006) *Thatcher*, London: Hodder Arnold.

Hayek, F. (1960) *The constitution of liberty*, London: Routledge.

Hayek, F. (1988) *The fatal conceit: The errors of socialism*, London: Routledge.

Heffer, S. (2010a) 'General election 2010: David Cameron had this coming to him', *Daily Telegraph* (http://www.telegraph.co.uk/news/election-2010/7692564/General-Election-2010-David-Cameron-has-had-this-coming-to-him.html).

Heffer, S. (2010b) 'Only a Tory without principles would demonise the Right', *Daily Telegraph* (http://www.telegraph.co.uk/comment/columnists/simonheffer/7737948/Only-a-Tory-without-principles-would-demonise-the-Right.html).

Heffer, S. (2010c) 'David Cameron will rue the day he betrayed the Conservatives', *Daily Telegraph* (http://www.telegraph.co.uk/comment/columnists/simonheffer/7750235/David-Cameron-will-rue-the-day-he-betrayed-the-Conservatives.html).

Hegel, G. (1991) *Elements of the philosophy of Right*, Cambridge: Cambridge University Press.

Heidegger, M. (1962) *Being and time*, Oxford: Blackwell.

Heilbrunn, J. (2008) *They knew they were right: The rise of the neocons*, New York: Doubleday.

HM Treasury (2010a) *Budget 2010*, London: HM Treasury.

HM Treasury (2010b) *Spending Review 2010*, London: HM Treasury.

Honderich, T. (1990) *Conservatism*, London: Hamish Hamilton.

Jenkins, S. (1995) *Accountable to none: The Tory nationalisation of Britain*, London: Hamish Hamilton.

Jones, D. (2008) *Cameron on Cameron: Conversations with Dylan Jones*, London: Fourth Estate.

Katwala, S. (2006) 'The genius of Simon Heffer', *The Guardian* (http://www.guardian.co.uk/commentisfree/2006/mar/30/thegeniusofsimonheffer).

Kekes, J. (1998) *A case for Conservatism*, Ithaca: Cornell University Press.

King, A. (2010a) 'So why didn't the Tories reach the summit?', *Daily Mail* (http://www.dailymail.co.uk/debate/election/article-1274795/UK-ELECTION-RESULTS-2010-So-didnt-Tories-reach-summit).

King, P. (2010b) *Housing policy transformed: The right to buy and the desire to own*, Bristol: The Policy Press.

King, P. (2010c) *Housing boom and bust: Owner occupation, government regulation and the credit crunch*, London: Routledge.

Kirk, R. (1986) *The Conservative mind: From Burke to Eliot*, 7th revised edition, Washington: Regnery Press.

Kristol, I. (1995) *Neo-Conservatism: The autobiography of an idea*, New York: The Free Press.

Lebrun, R. (1988) *Joseph de Maistre: An intellectual militant*, Kingston and Montreal: McGill-Queen's University Press.

Lee, A. (2010) 'Hundreds of BBC viewers left furious after Eastenders ditched for Gordon Brown's resignation speech', *Metro*, 18 May (http://www.metro.co.uk/tv/826213-hundreds-of-bbc-viewers-left-furious-after-eastenders-ditched-for-gordon-brown-s-resignation-speech).

Liberal Democrats (2010) *Changes that work for you: Building a fairer Britain*, London: Liberal Democrats.

Maistre, J. de (1850) *The Pope: Considered in his relations with the Church, temporal sovereignties, separated churches and the cause of civilisation*, London: Dolman.

Maistre, J. de (1974) *Considerations on France*, Kingston and Montreal: McGill-Queen's University Press.

Maistre, J. de (1993) *St. Petersburg dialogues: Or conversations on the temporal government of providence*, Kingston and Montreal: McGill-Queen's University Press.

Maistre, J. de (1996) *Against Rousseau*, Kingston and Montreal: McGill-Queen's University Press.

Maistre, J. de (1998) *An examination of the philosophy of Bacon: Wherein different questions of rational philosophy are treated*, Kingston and Montreal: McGill-Queen's University Press.

Marshall, P. and Laws, D. (eds) (2004) *The Orange Book: Reclaiming liberalism*, London: Profile Books.

McCue, J. (1997) *Edmund Burke and our present discontents*, London: Claridge Press.

Mises, L. (1981) *Socialism: An economic and social analysis*, Indianapolis: Liberty Fund.

Montgomerie, T. (2010) *Falling short: The key factors that contributed to the Conservative Party's failure to win a parliamentary majority*, London: ConservativeHome.

Muller, J. (1997) 'Introduction: what is Conservative social and political thought?', in J. Muller (ed) *Conservatism: An anthology of social and political thought from David Hume to the present*, Princeton: Princeton University Press, pp 3–31.

Nelson, F. and Forsyth, J. (2010) 'The manifesto is what we believe in, that is what matters', *The Spectator*, 1 May, pp 12–13.

Oakeshott, M. (1962) *Rationality in politics and other essays*, new and expanded edition, Indianapolis: Liberty Press.

O'Hara, J. (2010) *A new American tea party: The counterrevolution against bailouts, handouts, reckless spending, and more taxes*, New Jersey: Wiley.

O'Hara, K. (2005) *After Blair: Conservatism beyond Thatcher*, Cambridge, Icon.

O'Hear, A. (1999) *After progress: Finding the old way forward*, London: Bloomsbury.

O'Keeffe, D. (2010) *Edmund Burke*, London: Continuum.

Paulson, H. (2010) *On the brink: Inside the race to stop the collapse of the global financial system*, New York: Business Press.

Quinton, A. (1993) 'Conservatism', in P. Goodin and P. Pettit (eds) *A companion to contemporary political philosophy*, Oxford: Blackwell, pp 244–68.

Ramsden, J. (1998) *An appetite for power: A history of the Conservative Party since 1830*, London: Harper Collins.

Ratzinger, J. and Pera, M. (2006) *Without roots: The West, relativism, Christianity, Islam*, New York: Basic Books.

Roberts, A. (1999) *Salisbury: Victorian Titan*, London: Weidenfeld & Nicholson.

Schmidtz, D. (2002) 'Introductions', in D Schmidtz (ed) *Robert Nozick*, Cambridge: Cambridge University Press, pp 1–9.

Scruton, R. (1994) *The classical vernacular: Architectural principles in an age of nihilism*, Manchester: Carcenet.

Scruton, R. (2000) *England: An elegy*, London: Chatto and Windus.

Scruton, R. (2001) *The meaning of Conservatism* (3rd edn), Basingstoke: Palgrave.

Scruton, R. (2007) *Culture counts: Faith and feeling in a world besieged*, New York: Encounter Books.

Scruton, R. (2009) *Beauty*, Oxford: Oxford University Press.

Scruton, R. (2010) *The uses of pessimism: And the danger of false hope*, London: Atlantic Books.

Selbourne, D. (1994) *The principle of duty: An essay on the foundations of civic order*, London: Sinclair-Stevenson.

Snowdon, P. (2010) *Back from the brink: The inside story of the Tory resurrection*, London: Harper Press.

Stephens, P. (2010) 'A struggle btween new and old politics', *Financial Times*, May 10, p 3.

Sternhell, Z. (2010) *The anti-Enlightenment*, New Haven, CT: Yale University Press.

Waltson, P. (2010) *The German genius: Europe's third renaissance, the second scientific revolution and the twentieth century*, London: Simon & Schuster.

Williams, H. (1998) *The guilty men: Conservative decline and fall, 1992–1997*, London: Aurum Press.

Wittgenstein, L. (1953) *Philosophical investigations*, Oxford: Blackwell.

Index

THE NEW POLITICS
Liberal Conservatism or same old Tories?

Peter King

First published in Great Britain in 2011 by

The Policy Press
University of Bristol
Fourth Floor
Beacon House
Queen's Road
Bristol BS8 1QU
UK

Tel +44 (0)117 331 4054
Fax +44 (0)117 331 4093
e-mail tpp-info@bristol.ac.uk
www.policypress.co.uk

North American office:
The Policy Press
c/o International Specialized Books Services (ISBS)
920 NE 58th Avenue, Suite 300
Portland, OR 97213-3786, USA
Tel +1 503 287 3093
Fax +1 503 280 8832
e-mail info@isbs.com

© The Policy Press 2011

British Library Cataloguing in Publication Data
A catalogue record for this book is available from the British Library.

Library of Congress Cataloging-in-Publication Data
A catalog record for this book has been requested.

ISBN 978 1 84742 853 0 paperback
ISBN 978 1 84742 854 7 hardcover

The right of Peter King to be identified as author of this work has been asserted by him
in accordance with the 1988 Copyright, Designs and Patents Act.

Cover design by The Policy Press
Front cover: image kindly supplied by www.alamy.com
Printed and bound in Great Britain by TJ International, Padstow
The Policy Press uses environmentally responsible print partners.

MIX
Paper from
responsible sources
FSC® C013056